By John Wright

WILLOW CREEK

An Imprint of NorthWord Press, Inc.

Box 1360, Minocqua, WI 54548

Library of Congress Cataloging-in-Publication Data

Wright, John, 1948 –
    Trout on a stick / by John Wright – 1st ed.
       p.   cm.
    ISBN 1-55971-11-6 : $14.95
     1. Outdoor cookery. 2. Cookery (Game)   3. Cookery (Fish)
  I. Title.
TX823.W75   1991
641.5′78 – d20   91-12071
                                            CIP

Published in the United States
by Willow Creek Press,
an imprint of NorthWord Press, Inc.
P.O. Box 1360, Minocqua, WI 54548

For a free color catalog describing
NorthWord's line of books and gift items,
call 1-800-336-5666.

Designed by Origins Design, Inc.
Typesetting by Cavanaugh Ink.

Printed in Singapore
ISBN 1-55971-111-6

First Edition

Contents

Foreword & Acknowledgments

Trout On a Stick is part cookbook, part comic book, and part outdoor adventure book. The stories are as true as my memory is accurate.

Most of the recipes have a story to go with them. Some of the incidents were funny at the time they occurred, some only seem funny now. The majority of the recipes will make for pretty good grub, though you'll note that a few fall into the category of "don't do this!" These are things I learned not to fix the hard way — like sagebrush stew, for instance. But I'm getting my packsaddle ahead of my mule. You'll see for yourself as we go along.

Right here I'd like to say thanks, one and all, to everybody who helped this book come to life. That includes all the good folks I've hunted and fished with, packed in with, cooked for, or with whom I maybe just shared a camp, drink, or a good story.

Most of all, I want to thank Shirley, my wife and biggest fan, for planting the seed of this idea in my head and then doing all she could to help it grow. Thanks, sweetie, this one's for you!

I'd also be sadly remiss if I neglected to credit the fine people who did so much to help and support me during the writing and search for a publisher of this book. I've already mentioned my wife Shirley, to whom the book is dedicated. She proved to be an able typist and first line editor. And many thanks to:

Don and Joyce Tollman, unofficial literary agents and great friends. Henry Gross, former Executive Editor for Outdoor Life Books, and the first man of letters to take an interest in my work. Martin Meyers, old Tahoe Pardner and the man who infected me with fly fishing fever. Big Mike . . . who's always there. Glenn Law, Montana hunting and fishing buddy and outdoor writer of some stature, for his blistering encouragement. My brother Jeff, a fine artist who de-mystified for me the use of color inks. Russell Chatham, for sharing his great duck recipe. Gail Rich, whose positive energy was a powerful force. My aunt Ida Belle, a sweet little southern lady who put hope in my heart and beans on my table. Allen Reynolds, the "Honorable Man of Music Row," whose good advice kept me on a straight course. And last but in no way least, to the man who remembered, the man who, for me, symbolizes the motto "Do the Right Thing," Ranger Chuck.

Now, saddle up and ride along. I hope you enjoy the trip.

Chef Shedhorn
a.k.a. John Wright

Rules of the Road:
Some Thoughts on Hunting

A lot of folks take a pretty dim view of hunting and hunters these days. That's a shame, because sometimes it puts friends on two sides of a fence. It has happened to me.

I grew up in a family where hunting was a time-honored tradition and a natural rite of passage for a boy into young manhood. It was a way to teach responsibility through safe gun handling, consideration for others by way of observing rights of property owners, and love of nature by learning the habits of wildlife. It was also a strengthening of the bond between my Dad and myself.

I think the big problem facing the legitimate hunter today is the effect of the "rotten apple syndrome." That's the one where a handful of no-account S.O.B.s with guns tear around the countryside drinking, trespassing, shooting up road signs, cutting fences, and pretty thoroughly ruining public relations for those of us who know how to behave afield.

So why do we hunt? Killing is only a small part of the experience. A climax. True, a clean kill and a skillful shot are two desired elements of the experience, but that's just the icing on the cake. The cake is the hunt itself, the preparation for the hunt, and the aftermath — the great dinners of wild game and, of course, the memories of beautiful days, good shooting, of proud dogs making courageous retrieves.

The more days I spend afield, the less important it is for me to bring home a full game bag. To see and hear a marsh come to life with the rising sun, to sit a good horse on a high and windy ridge, or to just walk through a patch of bird cover with a well balanced double-barreled gun and a good dog . . . that's plenty.

If you're a hunter, I hope you feel this way, too. If you're not, I hope that maybe you can understand.

Rules of the Road:
About Trout

I'd like to make a statement here about trout fishing and trout eating. Despite the title of this book, I am pretty much a catch and release advocate where trout are concerned, especially stream and river trout. Trout in lakes are not subjected to as many threats to their survival, so I'm more likely to keep a few "eaters" when lake fishing.

In the last ten years or so, the so-called "blue ribbon" trout streams of the West have seen a tremendous increase in fishing pressure. Creel limits have been reduced in many instances, but that doesn't completely relieve the effects of constant assaults by fishermen. For that reason, I'd like to propose this ethic for keeping or releasing trout: Except for a few small trout, say ten inches or under, release your catch when stream fishing. Occasionally a fish will swallow a fly, become foul hooked, or otherwise injure itself to the point of not surviving. By all means, keep that fish so as not to waste it.

In mountain lakes the situation is different. Pressure is usually less, and some lakes are overpopulated to the point of the fish becoming stunted. You need not feel guilty about keeping enough for a feed — within the legal limit, of course.

Now about trophy fish. Everybody wants to hang a big one over the fireplace, and there's nothing wrong with having a reminder of a great day on the water and a gallant fight well won. But you can have that now without killing a trophy fish. A number of taxidermists can now build you an exact replica of your fish, using color photos and measurements you take in the field. These mounts are constructed of synthetic materials and are much more durable than conventionally mounted fish, which are organic and doomed to deterioration.

So I'm asking you to put 'em back alive when you can. Millions of fly fishermen will thank you, and the next time you meet that fish, he'll be much bigger!

One more thing: When you have a good fish on, don't play him to the point of exhaustion. Bring him on in, and if he gets off, at least you know he'll survive. Also, when releasing a trout, don't just pitch him back in like a chunk of stove wood. Hold him as gently as possible, head into the current, rocking him up and back 'til he starts to squirm. Then just open your hands and watch him slip into the shadows.

And finally, please use only barbless hooks.

DREAMS OF A MOUNTAIN MAN

Rules of the Road:
Junk Food

Everybody knows that you can't climb around the mountains day after day on a diet of chips, soda pop, candy bars and other processed foodstuffs. However, if you put three squares of well-balanced chow on the camp dining table, I think a little junk food in camp can still be a good thing.

Most of your guests these days, whether hunters, fishermen, family campers, photography buffs, or others, are used to a few processed items in their diet. At times, going on a pack trip where such food is totally unavailable can cause a state of mild withdrawal in some individuals. That fact is that any problem you have in the mountains is magnified beyond flat land dimensions.

If you're packing in with horses and mules, you have the option of carrying a few non-essentials. Most folks seem to crave sweets and fatty foods at high altitudes, so here are some things that pack well and travel durably.

1. Chips such as Pringles™, which are packed in canisters, like tennis balls.

2. Hard candies like lemon drops and jelly beans.

3. Durable candy bars such as Snickers™, Heath Bars™, and so on, that are packed in cartons.

4. Canned sodas. Most people leave diets down on the flats, so unless requested, leave the diet drinks down there, too.

5. Cookies packed in tins.

If there are kids in camp, you need to watch their intake of this stuff. Beyond that, just be sure you put plenty of good solid chuck in front of your guests. Then, if they eat all their veggies, you can give them a treat.

The Cast of Characters:
Chef Shedhorn

An old friend and outfitter from Ennis, Montana, name of Wade Durham, has his main elk camp on Shedhorn Creek in the Madison Range. It's a top-notch camp and he puts his hunters on to a lot of good bulls and some big buck deer.

The year that I was Wade's camp cook, the first bunch of hunters we had were a real good-humored lot. They enjoyed camp life, all bagged decent elk, and made me feel like a Cordon bleu chef.

One of the guides jokingly referred to me as "Chef Shedhorn" one night, because the camp was situated on Shedhorn Creek. Well, the hunters picked it up, and then the outfitter and the other guides. Pretty soon I had a nickname.

By the way, the creek gets its name from the fact that a good number of elk winter at the top end of the drainage there rather than migrating down to the valley below. That's because Shedhorn Mountain, a long, bald ridge, is blown clear of snow by winter winds, and the elk can stay and feed 'til spring on the exposed grass. This means that the bulls are concentrated when the time comes to shed their antlers. Thus the name Shedhorn Creek.

So that's how Chef Shedhorn got his name, and I'm proud of it.

The Cast of Characters:
Packers

Here's to the packer, the unsung hero of the mountains. Packing is an art form, no mistake, and truly good packers are scarce these days. In frontier times, before wagon roads, all goods came and went by pack train. The packer did his share to help build this country. In remote wilderness areas, they're still doing their part today.

Pictured here are the brothers Durham, Wade and Todd. Wade is the one standing on the stump. The load they're building looks mighty tall, but it'll cinch down as they draw up their hitch rope. The horse, name of Blue, does double duty as a riding and pack animal.

Operating a pack string day after day, going countless miles on rough trails and keeping your stock sound takes a lot of savvy. You must be a master of knots and hitches, horse psychologist, horse shoer, veterinarian, and a good physical specimen to boot. Physically, it's a very demanding job.

If you go on a pack trip to the mountains, take time to show your packer you appreciate him. He's the one who gets your gear in and out in good shape, and you can't go without him.

The Cast of Characters: Mountain Horses

The main ingredient for any mountain pack trip is a good saddle horse. You can have the best equipment, the best pack string, and be camped in the prettiest spot on earth, but if you're poorly mounted, you'll not enjoy yourself much.

This picture is of a mare I rode for a season in Montana, and she has many of the qualities you look for in a good mountain horse. First, she's hell for stout with a broad chest, deep heart girth, and muscular hind quarters. With good bone, her legs tend toward being a little short. A tall horse is stylish until you find yourself picking your way through the timber, ducking low-hanging limbs laden with snow. It's also easier to mount up in deep snow while wearing chaps, gun belt, hunting knife and extra cartridges if your horse is not so tall. An old cowboy motto goes: "Admire the tall and saddle the small."

This particular mare had tremendous endurance. On several occasions I put twenty or more hard miles on her in a day and had as much horse under me when I got in as when I rode out.

As for looks she's not much, but with four-footed ladies as well as with the two-legged, beauty's only skin deep.

The Cast of Characters:
Guides

If you hire an outfitter to take you to the hills on a pack trip, whether for hunting, fishing, or just relaxation and photography, you should have a guide to make your trip a good one. For big game hunting, there should be no more than two hunters per guide. One on one is better but usually costs more. On fishing or photo trips, one good guide can handle a whole party if there are not more than, say, half a dozen.

A guide has to wear a lot of hats. He should be a horseman and be used to handling inexperienced riders without seeming like a coach. He needs to be a naturalist with practical knowledge of wildlife and local vegetation. First aid training is a must, and he needs highly developed survival skills.

He ought to be a passable good shot because too often his hunter is not, and it's his job to keep a wounded animal from suffering. Some guides I know carry only a sidearm, others a rifle. I carry both, the handgun as a backup to the rifle. I'm a "belt-and suspenders" man.

Most of all, the guide needs to be a good listener. In the mountains, formalities soon disappear and you can find yourself in the role of confidant to someone you've known only a couple of days. The guide should never make his client feel like a tenderfoot or refer to him as a "dude." The client pays good money to go packing, and if he wants to feel like more of a mountain man than he is, he's bought the privilege. If all the folks that go to the hills come out with a good feeling, then maybe the wilderness will last longer.

One more thing. The only reason your guide is there is because he loves the mountains and camp life. If figured by the hour, his pay probably wouldn't even come up to minimum wage. His day is seldom less than twelve hours long, sometimes twenty. If he's worth a damn, he honestly enjoys helping you enjoy yourself, so give him every break you can. Help him with the camp chores, he'll respect you for it. Take his instructions without argument, he knows his job. Give him credit for being a professional, and, in a week or ten-day trip, you may find you've made a friend for life.

And if he does his job and you get your game or the fishing is good or you just generally have a good trip, show your appreciation with a tip. As I said before, the pay ain't much, and with a little extra from you he can keep on doing the job he loves.

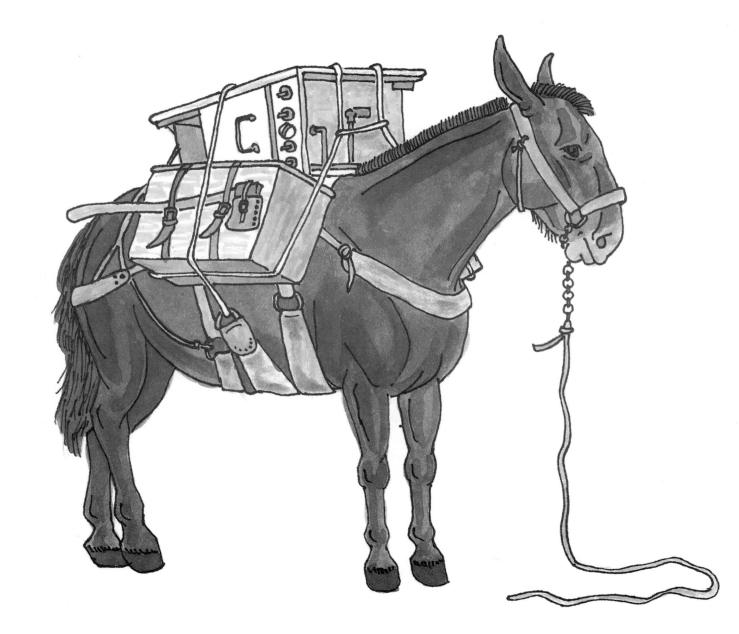

The Cast of Characters:
Mules

It has been my privilege and pleasure to have been associated with some very good mules over the years, and a few not so good. (I believe that the bad ones were made that way by harsh breaking methods or rough handling.)

A good mule is valuable beyond measure. Pictured here is Liz, and she is standing quietly with one hundred and fifty pounds of propane range on her back. I can't tell you what a luxury that stove was to me as a camp cook, and I'll never be able to thank her enough for packing it in. On twenty miles of rough trail in the mountains, she never so much as rubbed a tree trunk. She is one good mule.

Mules also make good saddle mounts. They have a different gait than a horse, almost a shuffle, and they are very smooth even on rough terrain. One fellow I cooked and packed for has a riding mule named Ted. Ted is tall and handsome and his back has never felt a pack. Ted's owner is not poor, and I doubt there's enough money in the state of Montana to buy that mule.

A word of caution regarding mules: If you know a mule to be a kicker, give him a wide berth. A mule is so fast and accurate that a Karate master looks crippled by comparison. He won't even bother to try for you unless he knows you're in range and he just won't miss. So, if a mule is bad and you know it, give that south end plenty of respect. I want to stress, though, that bad mules are made, not born. Hardly ever, anyway.

Mules are not only more sure footed than horses, they have more sense as well. A horse when spooked may panic, hurting himself as well as you if you're aboard. A mule, however, has a more level head and a higher opinion of himself. He'll almost never do anything that will endanger himself, and that's good news for you if you're riding or packing him.

I hope you have the chance to get acquainted with some good mules some day. You'll be surprised how much company they can be in camp as well as a great help in packing meat and gear. But if you keep your mules in a corral, build it high, 'cause they jump like frogs!

Trout On a Stick

This may be the easiest and best recipe in the book. I got it in Montana, where I lived for six and a half years. It originated when I had a mess of golden trout and no skillet to fry them in. Here's how it was.

One summer a few years back, I went on a day ride with a young lady. Our route took us up to a high mountain lake in a little cirque, or basin. The elevation was about 10,000 feet and the lake held eight- and ten-inch golden trout in great abundance. They acted like they hadn't eaten for a week, and we wore 'em out.

We kept enough for a good feed, but how to cook our catch? It was time to improvise. All we'd brought were our horses and fly rods. I dug around in my saddlebags and found a plastic bag with some salt in it. There was a lemon rolling around in there too, and sticks were in good supply. This is how we did it.

INGREDIENTS: Pan-sized trout; salt; lemon juice; green sticks.

1. **Build your fire of dry dead limbs. Let them burn down to coals.**

2. **Clean trout with the heads on; salt the body cavity.**

3. **Shave the bark off a green limb and sharpen the point. Spit trout on stick through the mouth, embedding point in meat of the trout's tail.**

4. **Cook over coals like a hot dog 'til skin blisters and peels, about ten minutes.**

5. **Peel skin off, douse with lemon juice, salt to taste.**

6. **Leaving trout on stick, eat meat off bones. Flip skeleton in fire.**

7. **Do another one.**

Scott's Once a Week Coffee

If you've ever spent a few days in a mountain hunting camp, above or below zero, you know the importance of good, strong coffee and plenty of it. You might get by with so-so chow, but the coffee's got to be right!

Montana guide and good friend Scott Wallace, one of the best hands in the mountains I ever met, showed me the easiest way to make camp coffee I know. He also showed me (great practical joker) how to sink a horse apple in a cup of coffee to serve to special friends.

Anyway, we had packed into the Sapphire Range in western Montana and set up camp for the first night. When the horses and mules were picketed and fed, Scott built a fire and made coffee. Like this:

INGREDIENTS: Gallon coffee pot (no innards); spring or creek water; coffee.

After bringing a gallon of creek water to a boil in a blue granite campfire pot, he threw in two handfuls of coffee and brought it back to a boil. Then he set it to one side to steep. After about ten minutes, he poured in half a cup of cold water to settle the grounds. That was it and the coffee was outstanding.

But like Paul Harvey says, "Here's the rest of the story." Good coffee doesn't last long in camp, and with seven guys in this one, the pot was empty in no time. I went to dump the grounds for another batch and almost got myself shot. "Hold on!" Scott hollered, and filled the pot again without removing the grounds. Then he boiled it and threw in only one handful of coffee. "You keep doing this 'till the pot's plum full up with grounds. Then when you can't get any more water in, it's time to dump it out. All this takes the best part of a week."

Hence the name, Once a Week coffee. It makes the finest tasting coffee I ever had, pot after pot, not bitter at all. I've served it to some mighty picky hunters and always got good reviews. If it doesn't sound to you like it will work, just try. But if you chicken out and change the grounds too soon, I can't be held responsible for the results.

Cabin Fever Coffeecake

A bit southeast of Lake Tahoe, California, at about 9,000 feet elevation, lies a little mountain valley known locally as Miess's Meadow. In that valley, beside the creek stands a cabin. At least I sure hope it's still standing, because if it isn't, I'd be heart-broken. It's been there a lot of seasons, and some of the best times I ever had were spent under its roof. It's where this recipe originated.

I don't know who built the cabin, but the Forest Service owns it now and leases it as a cow camp along with grazing rights in the valley. It shows up elsewhere in this book with the recipe for Jim Henry's Skillet Spuds.

Snug and cozy, the little house stands two stories, with wood shingles for siding and roof. It's built with the back door hanging out over an eddy in the creek, sort of cantilevered. There used to be a little milk can on a rope that you could toss out the door into the pool, and so get your water without leaving the kitchen. A wood range stands in the center of the one room downstairs, which serves for both cooking and heating. It's a camp cook's heaven.

Along with friends, I used to head for that cabin every chance I got, year round. We'd go in on horseback during the summer and fall, to fish and hunt, and in the winter we'd ski in, entering the cabin by way of the second story window. Ten feet of snow drifted against the walls made for good insulation.

The fall of 1972 brought another deer season, and with two carpenter buddies I rode into Miess's Meadow and the little shack below the peaks. We'd no sooner got unpacked and gotten the horses staked out in the sun-cured grass, than it began to snow. And snow. As the flakes came down, so did the temperature.

We put up a good slug of wood, enough for several days. After the horses were well grazed, we tied them in the shed beside the cabin. The snow continued, and it got colder. With the sundown came a stiff wind, but the wood range kept the cabin toasty. The steaks we'd brought for first night's supper went down easy, and following a brief discussion of prospective hunting strategies, all hands hit their bunks.

Cabin Fever Coffeecake

Next morning it was snowing sideways. The thermometer tacked to the door frame said five degrees above. Determined to make an effort, we bundled up, saddled up and took a scout around. An hour later, having spotted nothing, we dismounted at the cabin door, frozen stiff as hammer handles. Firing the wood range to a rosy glow, we spent the rest of the day playing cards. And the next day.

It wasn't long before we all showed classic symptoms of that dread disease, cabin fever. Boredom, restlessness, irritability: we had it all. The sky was like lead, and the light so flat that you couldn't tell the time without your watch. The atmosphere was surreal. Once I woke from a nap and started supper at two o'clock in the afternoon. It was kinda strange.

The card games were endless, and we played every game we knew. Spades was a challenge, because to play spades you must keep score, and we had no pencil. In a blinding flash of inventiveness, I used the exposed lead tip of a bullet to write on a paper plate. Honest.

Until the third day of our hunt we'd seen no tracks on our scouting rides. But on that last day's patrol we saw enough tracks for a herd of buffalo — only they were those of deer — leaving the valley and headed down country. The severe weather had prompted the winter migration, and our hunt was over. The game had quit the country while we slept.

We decided to roll our beds and pull out the next morning. Wayne and Jerry were visibly disappointed at our poor luck. I was too, but, determined to leave camp on an upscale note, I kicked out the stops and fixed a jam-up last night's supper. Dessert was in order, and I thought coffee cake would wash down well. Between the leftover food we'd packed in and what I found in the cabin cupboard, I was able to assemble a fair to middlin' coffeecake. And here it is:

Cabin Fever Coffeecake

INGREDIENTS: *2 cups Bisquick™ (or your own bagged biscuit mix); 1 cup granola (There are as many different types of granola as flies on a dead horse. Pick your favorite.); 1/3 cup raisins; 1/4 stick margarine or butter; 1/4 cup brown sugar; 1 1/2 teaspoons powdered cinnamon; milk or water to bind.*

Mix Bisquick™ and granola dry. When well blended, add milk or water (milk's better) and stir until you have a stiff dough. Powder your hands in a little of the Bisquick™ to keep the dough from sticking, and form dough into a round loaf. Scatter the raisins evenly across the top and punch them down in the dough a little ways. Place loaf in a greased iron skillet and bake in a 350 degree oven for about ten minutes or until it begins to brown. Remove from oven and take butter, which you've softened on the stove top, and spread it over the top of the loaf evenly. Then sprinkle the sugar and cinnamon over all. Pop back in oven for five or six more minutes. Serves three or four, depending on appetites.

Shipman's Pocket Dog Chips

Here's another easy one from Montana. About eight years ago, my son and I were elk hunting with Robin Shipman, an old friend from bachelor days. We were riding out of Robin's outfitter's camp, glassing parks and ridges for elk or sign of them. Lunchtime came. We ate the sandwiches we'd packed, and continued to hunt throughout the afternoon.

It was a great day and a good ride, but we didn't spot any game. A little before dark we were headed for camp, but still a good piece away. My stomach was growling and supper would be a long time coming. Justin, who was eight at the time, mentioned being hungry too. Robin pulled a plastic bag from his pocket. "Here," he offered, "have one of these dog t—-ds." Decorum prevents me from spelling it out, so I'll refer to it as a dog chip, as in buffalo chip.

And that's what it looked like, though in fact it was a hamburger patty, but more round, like a meatball. We each took one and went to work on them. It was about minus five degrees and the patties were partially

frozen, but real tasty and filling. Just the thing for a trail snack. They got us to camp in fine shape, and we were glad to have them. You make them like this:

INGREDIENTS: Ground beef (venison or elk works, too); garlic powder; black pepper; chopped onion; salt; any other spices you might like.

1. Break up meat and season to taste.

2. Chop and saute onions and sprinkle over meat.

3. Mix all ingredients and form into round patties like meatballs.

4. Pan fry, well done — they travel better that way.

5. Take a pocketful hunting, fishing, hiking, whatever.

Sagebrush Stew

Sit back and get comfortable — there's quite a tale goes with this one. Ten or eleven years back, when I was still single and living in southwest Montana, a local so-called outfitter asked me to guide for him on his first elk hunt of the season. I had never guided for him before and didn't really know him very well. If I had, none of this would ever have taken place. Needless to say, the alleged outfitter shall remain unnamed.

The trouble was, I'd never set one foot in this fellow's hunting area, didn't even know where the trailhead was to go in on. In addition to that, the guy's camp was only half set up and he wasn't going to be there. "That's no problem," he had said, "this first bunch knows I'm not really ready for them. I told them I couldn't take them in for opening day 'cause camp wasn't set up right. But they say they don't care, they want to hunt. Plus, I'm giving 'em a discount, and Robin knows the country. He'll get you lined out."

That sounded like it might work, so I agreed. I caught my mare and hauled her to town where Robin (see Recipe #3) and I loaded gear in the trucks, brought the rest of the pack and riding stock in from the pasture, and got ready to take the hunters in the following day.

Next morning broke crisp and clear. We loaded the horses and mules, then headed up the road to meet the hunters at the trailhead. Things sort of went downhill from there. A good ways down, to say the least, as we'll soon see.

Our eager clients were there at the trailhead parking lot, hanging around their truck, waiting for something to happen. As I later found out, all three were from Pennsylvania and all three were cement finishers. Their ages were late twenties to late thirties.

They were a dubious-looking outfit. The youngest one stood maybe 5 foot 9 inches and had to weigh at least 300 pounds, maybe more. From here on, we'll call him Big Boy #1. The next fellow, in between in age and weight, went about 230 pounds and was between 30 and 35 years old. He'll be Big Boy #2. Last but not least was the only one under 200 pounds. He was around 40 years old, and I'll refer to him as Slim.

They didn't look much like hunters and they sure didn't look like horsemen. To top it off, they had a girl with them who looked to be about eighteen or nineteen, had an impressive body, and seemed to be somewhat addled. I never heard a word pass her lips

Sagebrush Stew

the whole time we were in the hills. Big Boy #2 spoke up and claimed her as his wife. She never said, one way or the other.

We got the stock saddled and packed and Robin drove back to town. Aside from Big Boy #1 almost pulling his horse off its feet when he mounted (with help), the ride was uneventful. The trail followed the creek, and camp was in a typically beautiful northern Rockies setting. By the time we had the mules unpacked, it was supper time.

This brings us to our cook. The so-called outfitter had dug up a nineteen-year-old kid from town who had never so much as fried an egg. You begin to get the picture? Mercifully, that first night's supper was prepared in town by a real cook and brought in cold, to reheat in a hurry. It was the last edible meal we had for some time. Like the self-proclaimed outfitter, this alleged cook shall remain anonymous.

Opening day breakfast was an abomination. Rare bacon, swimming in grease, and eggs fried so hard they resembled credit cards. All washed down with either coffee, or industrial solvent — I couldn't tell. It set the tone for what was about to follow.

Robin, being familiar with the country, was supposed to ride in at daylight, get me headed out properly, and take one of the hunters with him. Daylight came. Robin didn't. Still no Robin by eight o'clock in the morning. I killed all the time I could saddling up, but it soon became obvious I was stalling. Just as the cement finishers began to grumble, Robin's wife, Linda, greatly pregnant at the time, came riding into camp to report that Robin had some sort of stomach flu and couldn't make it. All she could tell me was that the trail up the mountain was to the southeast of camp.

So, I got Big Boy #1 on his horse, with the cook's help. When the mare saw him coming, she spread all fours like a camel getting down for a drink. Then, with the mud master in tow, I started my horse out of camp. We left the child bride standing, staring vacantly outside the cook tent.

The trail wound up the mountain, and I stopped periodically to get my bearings. "You don't know this country. You ain't been in here before!" That from Big Boy #2, and not said kindly. So much for the understanding between them and the outfitter.

In spite of all this, I located a bunch of about eight head of elk right away, and there were at least two good

Sagebrush Stew

bulls among them. We tied the horses and began moving up on foot. The elk were grazing on an open hillside and easing toward the timber. Trouble was, with my hunters as overweight as they were, we hadn't a chance of getting in range before the elk made the trees and disappeared. And that's what happened.

After much bad-mouthing of me and the outfitter, they agreed that Slim, the only one who was fit enough to climb, would go with me and try to over-take the elk. The other two would hunt the lower timber together and we'd meet up back at camp that evening. With that we split up.

Now it was up to ol' Slim and me. While he wasn't used to altitude, neither did he have to drag a bloated carcass around, so he managed to keep up, for the most part. At least I didn't have to pack his rifle.

We only saw one elk the rest of the day, a spike bull at about seven hundred yards, and there was no way to get closer without spooking him. It was a cross-canyon shot and much too far to attempt, but good ol' Slim didn't see it that way. He was carrying a 7 mm magnum, which in truth is a good long-range flat-shooting cartridge for elk. But seven hundred yards is a long poke. Too long. I had a hell of a time convincing

Slim of this. As a matter of fact, he never was convinced. I had to pull rank and forbid the shot.

Slim was sullen, but I didn't want a gut-shot elk in my dreams. He insisted on a stalk, but we were forced to expose our position before we'd covered fifty yards, and the bedded bull rose and lit out.

We worked our way back to the horses and discovered that the Big Boys' mounts were still there as well as ours. That meant the Big Boys were either lost or too lazy to backtrack for their horses. I figured it an even bet, but I won't say which I hoped for.

Slim and I mounted up and led the spare horses back to camp with us. After corralling and feeding all the stock, we entered the cook tent. The Big Boys were home from the hill and they were drunk and mad. This brings us to Recipe #4.

Part of the reason they were upset was the meal they'd been presented with. Our young cook had made an attempt at beef stew, and the resulting gruel was a loathsome mess. It's a fact that hunger is the best sauce, and I ate my portion, for I was starved, but it was truly awful. The only identifiable ingredients

Sagebrush Stew

were beef and potatoes. The stock looked like mud in the road. Also, there was the strong taste of sage.

So strong, in fact, that if I hadn't been ravenous, I couldn't have choked it down. Apparently the alleged cook thought the stew too bland and had heard somewhere that sage was a popular seasoning. As there were numerous sagebrush plants growing around camp, our young chef simply broke off a healthy green sprig and pitched it in the stewpot. The outcome was catastrophic.

While I forced down supper, Big Boy #2 filled himself with wind and more liquor, raving on about the lousy food, the miserable camp, the no-account guide, the S.O.B. outfitter, and a number of other gripes and bitches. His dull-eyed bride simply sat and stared and, like the tarbaby in the Uncle Remus stories, said nothing. Big Boy #1 grunted an occasional "Yeah" or "That's right" in agreement with Big Boy #2, especially the part about the bad food.

The more he drank, the more Big Boy #2 wound himself up. Finally he blurted, "We're going to shoot the horses for camp meat, hang the guide, and --- the

cook!" Good taste keeps me from being more specific, but his plans for our young chef included socially unacceptable acts. In an attempt to lighten the mood, I suggested they deal with the cook first and hang me afterwards, as I would like to witness the proceedings. The humor was lost on our guests.

As I was riding my own good mare, a thoroughbred-quarter-horse cross, I didn't want her shot for camp meat or any other reason. I also had no interest in being hanged. To tell the truth, I had small concern for the fate of the cook. My main worry was about the horse. It was time to ride.

I told Big Boy #2 that he wasn't going to shoot or hang anything or anybody and that I was going to ride out right then and talk to the outfitter and try and get their money back, then come in the next morning and pack them out. They finally agreed, so I saddled the mare and headed down-country. The moon was big, and the mare stepped out confidently.

Our cook was a little nervous at the thought of being left alone with our guests, but I was determined to get my horse out of harm's way. Besides, if they threatened him too seriously, he could always fix them something to eat.

Sagebrush Stew

The ride out was pleasant enough, considering the circumstances. The moon shown on the peaks and, as it was early in the season, it was not too cold. The mare was a real traveler, so it wasn't too long before we were at the trailhead and the parking lot.

I unsaddled and tied her to the horse trailer. The cook's Volkswagen was the only car available; the key was in the ashtray. When I finally got the car started, I headed for the highway. There was a steel gate at the end of the dirt road from the parking lot, and as I approached it I applied the brakes. There weren't any!

Frantically pumping the brakes, I geared down to slow the car. Right here I'd like to attest to the durability of Powder River brand gates. The VW hit the gate at between five and ten miles an hour and simply bounced back off of it. After regaining my composure, I got out and opened the gate and headed for town. The rest of the drive was uneventful.

At about one a.m. I pulled into the outfitter's driveway and managed to stop the car without hitting anything. The outfitter's wife answered the door and told me that he was over in the Gallatin Range, guiding a moose hunter. As I later found out, they were lost.

I told her about the crisis in camp and she agreed I should bring the hunters out in the morning, at which time she would refund their money. At that I went home and fell into bed for a couple of hours. It had been a long day. Sleep came easy.

I was at Robin's house at daybreak. He had two of his own horses in camp and, after hearing the story, was as anxious as I was to get back in to settle the situation. We drove to the trailhead in his pickup, which had brakes, and I saddled the mare. As we prepared to head up-country, Robin went behind the truck seat and produced two revolvers, a .357 magnum and a .44 magnum. He handed me the .357 and buckled the .44 on himself. As we started up the trail, the weight of the revolver was reassuring. I hated to think of actually having to use it, but we were approaching armed men who'd made grave threats.

We rode the mare by turns, and as we neared camp I imagined all sorts of things: horses on skewers, roasting above a low fire; the alleged cook staked out over a log; the tents in smoldering ruins.

When we caught sight of the camp, none of this had happened. Seeing the horses in the corral and on their

Sagebrush Stew

feet, I felt a small rush of relief. Our young cook was frying up a batch of his bulletproof eggs when we came in, and he too had armed himself. He looked terrified, a .22 pistol strapped over his apron. Apparently he'd managed to keep himself out of the Big Boys' clutches. He looked glad to see us, to say the least.

The Big Boys and Slim were doing a hung-over job of saddling the horses. After all the threats and big wind of the night before, they actually planned on going hunting. I told them that, on the contrary, the only ride they were taking was down the home trail. They protested, said they were sorry and so on. But after the night I'd had and little sleep, I was in a very unforgiving mood. I said as much. There was some grumbling, but the sight of our sidearms gave them to know that our intentions were serious.

To quote *Rawhide's* trail boss, we "headed 'em up and moved 'em out." As we neared the parking lot at the end of the trail, I saw grandpa Carl Hubner standing beside his pickup, holding his deer rifle at port arms. He was there to help us haul gear to town and he'd heard all about our trouble. Concerned for Robin and me, he later said that if the two of us hadn't come out of that canyon, he'd have shot everybody who did.

Grandpa was an in-law of Robin's and plenty salty. Looking back, I think he just might have done what he said. An old-time Montanan, grandpa Carl had an edge to him that was just as hard as the ground on which he stood.

Now I don't say that Sagebrush Stew caused all this trouble, but it helped. It's a definite "don't do," but just for the record, here's the recipe.

INGREDIENTS: Everything you put in your own beef stew, and one large green sprig of sage (off sagebrush).

1. **Prepare your usual beef stew recipe.**

2. **Throw in sagebrush sprig.**

3. **Simmer for one hour.**

4. **Remove from heat, let stand 'til cool.**

5. **Throw stew to the dogs (not your dogs), give the pot to the Salvation Army.**

NOTE: *If you should be self destructive enough to try to eat the results of this recipe, I refuse to be held in any way responsible for the outcome of such foolishness!*

Jim Henry's Skillet Spuds

Here's one I picked up in northern California, when I lived in the Sierras at Lake Tahoe. It was about fifteen years back or so, during the deer season, and I was hunting alone on horseback.

The area I was hunting was summer range for cattle, and the fall roundup was in progress. I'd had no luck, due to all the activity, I supposed, so I rode into the cow camp to see what was up.

As it turned out, the cow boss was shorthanded and, before I knew it, I was hired to help gather cattle. I didn't know much about cows, but I was mounted on a tough little quarter horse gelding. I suspect the cow boss hired the horse more than me. I ended up spending a week on the gather, and it was unforgettable.

Most of all I remember Jim Henry, a cowboy's cowboy — small, wiry, about 45 years old, and hard as a railroad spike. He was hired on as top hand and pretty much ran the show. I can see him now, spurring his big Appaloosa through the rocks, sparks flying from the horseshoes, as casual as though he were loping across a golf course. As he rode, his back was as straight as a ramrod.

I didn't learn a lot about cows that week, but I did some of the wildest riding of my life. In the morning we'd go up on the heights with binoculars and glass for cattle. When we located a few head, we'd ride down to them as quietly as we could. These cows had been running free all summer and they were wild as bucks. As soon as we showed up, they'd dive off into the black timber, and the chase was on.

You can't run cows for a week on one horse, so I had an alternate mount issued to me. He was a big, raw-boned gelding, sorrel with a blaze, and plenty fast. Short on manners but long on endurance, he loved to chase cows, straight up, straight down, jumping deadfalls, busting brush, all at breakneck speed. I just gave him his head and hung on. It was thrilling.

We stayed in an old cabin surrounded by rugged peaks. It was a classic mountain cow camp equipped with a wood stove for both heat and cooking. A day in the saddle at eight or nine thousand feet of elevation will put an appetite on you, and we ate like wolves. The main components of our larder were the staples of the cowman, beef and potatoes. It came my

Jim Henry's Skillet Spuds

turn to cook and I thought fried spuds would go good with our steaks, so I sliced some and commenced to cook 'em up. Ol' Jim cast a cold blue eye on the proceedings and finally shoved me aside and took command of the stove. And here's Jim Henry's Skillet Spuds. You'll have to go a long way to taste better taters.

INGREDIENTS: Potatoes; onions; garlic cloves; bacon; salt and pepper.

1. Fry bacon crisp, drain, and break into small pieces. Set aside.

2. Mince garlic, slice onions, and saute in bacon grease. Remove from skillet and set aside.

3. Slice potatoes in the round, about 1/2 inch thick. Dump in skillet with a little more bacon grease and brown both sides. Salt and pepper as you go.

4. Move the skillet to a cooler part of the stove if you're using a wood range. If you're cooking on a conventional range, turn heat to simmer. Now add onion and garlic.

5. Add a little water to make steam, cover skillet and simmer for 30 or 40 minutes, stirring often.

6. Uncover and add bacon pieces. Stir occasionally for five or ten more minutes. Serve hot.

One last thing about Jim Henry. He was a tough old bird but had a warm heart. I never saw him again after the roundup, but I count him as a friend. Wherever he is, I hope he's still riding ramrod straight. Good luck, Jim, you cook good spuds.

Pan Fried Venison Chops

This is my favorite cut of deer meat and my favorite way to fix it. It's the same as a pork chop, only venison. The meat needs to be aged for maximum tenderness and flavor. Depending on air temperature, I like to hang a deer for a week to ten days before butchering. Also, in addition to making a clean shot, the important thing is to get the carcass cooled out as quickly as possible after the kill. If you pay attention to these details, you'll always have excellent venison.

INGREDIENTS: Venison chops (two per serving) trimmed of all fat; salt; coarse-ground black pepper; garlic cloves; butter.

1. Melt butter in iron skillet. Get it hot enough to almost smoke.

2. Crush garlic cloves and rub a little into one side of chop. Salt and pepper same side. Place in skillet, seasoned side down.

3. Now season the "up" side while the first side browns.

4. Venison is tough and dry if overdone, so serve chops medium rare. When blood oozes to the surface of the meat, it's time to turn.

5. Wait for blood to surface again. Then, they're ready.

6. Serve hot from skillet with rice or potatoes and broccoli or other green vegetable.

THEY SAY BEANS CAN GIVE A MAN BAD WIND, BUT IT DON'T NEVER SEEM TO DO ME THATAWAY!
J. WRIGHT '87 ©

George's Red Beans

Here's another one from Lake Tahoe days. I got it from an old fishing and prowling buddy, name of George Crites. George and I squandered a significant portion of our youth together, and while he was mortally allergic to hard work, you couldn't have asked for a better fishing partner. On top of that, he was a laugh a minute.

Fourth of July at Lake Tahoe is a madhouse, and I always tried to get way back in the boonies on that weekend. One summer, I believe it was '72, George and I took that whole week and packed in to the headwaters of the Carson River. It was one of the two or three best trips I ever took, and we saw only one other horse outfit and two backpackers all week.

We simply fished our way upstream, day after day, and cutthroat trout in the eight-to-ten-inch range were in seemingly endless supply. Those were the days before I discovered the magic of the fly rod, and I'm ashamed to confess that neither was I a catch and release practitioner. Even so, we only killed enough for breakfast and supper each day, and they were superb.

Toward the middle of the week, we decided to take a side trip to a lake high up amongst the surrounding peaks, for it was rumored that monster trout were in residence there. It was a long, hot, dry ride with no grass or water along the trail. The horses got so tired and thirsty that we dismounted and walked the last couple of miles. The trail was very steep, and by the time we caught sight of the lake, horses and men were in a state of near collapse.

The lake was typically beautiful for the High Sierras, and grass grew lush along its shore. As this was the only feed available for several miles in any direction, and considering the seeming exhaustion of our saddle horses, I decided to leave them loose rather than picket them. We stripped off the saddles and bridles, left the halters on with the lead ropes to drag, and turned them out in the knee-high grass. They fell to grazing like it was a paying job.

Meanwhile, George and I made our spike camp by a tiny spring that formed a hat-sized basin, about fifty yards back from the lake's shore. George put his beans on to cook and we went fishing.

George's Red Beans

As you might have guessed, the "lake of the lunkers" that we almost killed ourselves and our mounts to get to was the only place we got skunked on the whole trip. We fished heroically 'til dark, but without effect. Apparently the lunkers did not exist or, more likely, our skills were somewhat lacking. In any case, we finally threw in the towel.

While George tended the beans, I checked on the horses. They both stood knee deep in the rich green grass and seemed content to stay put. I returned to the fire, following the aroma of bubbling red beans.

In the time it took for the beans to finish cooking, I whipped up a batch of biscuits. When all was ready, we dived in with a vengeance. After our rigorous day we were famished, and between the two of us we demolished the large pot of beans and all the biscuits. With swollen bellies and unhitched belts, we stoked up the fire and reared back to enjoy a smoke. It was then that I heard horse hooves on the trail. Headed home.

A little grass and water had affected a miraculous cure on the horses and they decided to mosey on down to the trailer, twenty-six miles away.

What followed was a panic stricken horse chase in the dark with badly overloaded bellies. This was not the first time I'd been deserted in the hills by four-legged companions, and I knew that if I didn't catch them, they'd walk as far back as they walked in, which was to the pickup and horse trailer. I didn't relish the idea of hoofing it out with a saddle and camp gear. Neither did George.

Every two hundred yards or so the horses would stop, only to take off again when they saw our flashlight coming. It was maddening. My stomach felt like it held a red hot bowling ball and I could hardly catch my breath. George was unable to keep up, so I took the flashlight and left him sitting in the pitch black timber.

By now I was mad and knew that I'd go all the way to the trailer before I came back empty-handed. The moon was out and I could see the horses up ahead, stopping and running, stopping and running. I was mad enough to bite a rock. I may have . . . I don't recall.

After about a mile and a half of this, I came up on them, stopped again. But instead of running, they just dumbly stood there, looking bored. I eased up to the

George's Red Beans

gelding and stroked his neck, and then I had his lead rope in my hand. The mare's lead was hung up in the sagebrush, and that's why they stopped. The gelding wouldn't leave her, so I had both of them.

I tied the end of the gelding's lead rope back around to the halter ring, hopped on bareback and led the mare back toward camp.

George was much relieved to see us as he had expected to have to spend the night on the trail. It was totally dark in the trees where he'd stopped, and there was no way to see the trail back to camp. He knew I'd go all the way down to the trailer if I had to, so the sight of us was a joyous one.

I'll not go into detail about the gastric effects of a moonlight jog with a belly full of beans, but I can assure you that nobody slept with their heads in their sleeping bags that night.

Anyhow, here's George's Red Beans, and if you like beans at all, you'll like them like this. No foolin', try 'em.

INGREDIENTS: 2 lbs pinto beans; onions; whole garlic cloves; $1/4$ lb. chunk salt pork (or a ham hock); one large bay leaf; tabasco sauce; salt; black pepper.

1. Soak beans overnight if you have time. If not, bring to a boil, then simmer 'til soft (2-3 hours).

2. Add salt pork, diced up, as soon as you begin to heat the beans.

3. Add bay leaf shortly after pork, leave whole so you can fish it out.

4. Continue to simmer. As stock forms, add $1/2$ teaspoon salt, plus 2 minced garlic gloves.

5. After beans have cooked two hours or are good and soft, add chopped onions, 1 teaspoon tabasco sauce, 1 teaspoon black pepper.

6. Simmer for another hour. Serve with biscuits or cornbread.

7. Now go check on your horses!

Greg's Eggs

This is an easy breakfast that I picked up in Montana the summer that I went through a guide and outfitter's school. My group of six students and our instructor had our base camp set up on the edge of the Sleeping Child Burn, where a huge fire had blackened thousands of acres years ago.

My friend Greg, who I pardnered up with during the school, and I decided to "spike out" one night. That meant leaving the base camp with one pack animal and the bare essentials for an overnight camp. Our gear consisted of a coffee pot and skillet, a little grub, and not much else. No tent, anyway, but since it was August and good weather, it didn't matter.

As we packed Ruby, the mule we'd been issued for the trip, our instructor, Scott (see Recipe #2), noticed us stuffing sleeping bags into the packsacks. "You wimps taking sleeping bags on a summer spike-out?" he asked.

"Sure," I answered. "Why not?"

"Well, hell!" he drawled. "No steely eyed mountain guide carries a sleeping bag on a spike-out in beautiful weather like this."

"So what do we sleep in?" Greg asked.

"Real mountain men just roll up in their manties," Scott scoffingly replied.

For those of you who've not packed in, a manty is a canvas sheet used over a packload and put on under the lash rope to keep sticks, dirt, rain and so forth out of your gear and grub. It's about seven feet square, like a small tarp. It doesn't make much of a blanket.

Nights had been warm, and since the whole crew was looking on, we wimps pulled the sleeping bags out of the pack and threw in an extra manty. With that, we saddled our horses and trailed out for Lake Abundance.

It was a six-mile ride through eye-popping northern Rocky Mountain terrain, and we enjoyed every foot of it.

Lake Abundance! The name conjures up pictures of leaping trout, endless meadows of lush graze for horses and mules, black timber poking the sky, and game in unlimited abundance. If it wasn't this good, it was close.

Greg's Eggs

The trail wound down from a high ridge, giving us a terrific view of the lake below and the meadow that bordered the creek. The trail was seldom traveled, and the last mile or so we had to jump deadfall timber every hundred yards. Moose tracks criss-crossed our path, the more so the closer we got to the lake. There was a little-used campsite hard by the water's edge, and it was sheltered by huge pine trees. We stripped the gear from the saddle horses and the mule, gathered up the night's firewood, and then turned our attention to the lake.

Joining my fly rod, I walked down to the water to see about something for supper. Greg was also a fly fisherman, but because he neglected to bring his outfit, he came along to serve as technical advisor.

By now the sun was behind the tree tops, and the surface of the lake was increasingly dimpled by rising trout. I tied on a Royal Wulff, a dry fly that looks like nothing in nature but is a proven trout producer. My personal opinion is that the trout, offended by the intrusion of a thing so out of character in their well-ordered world, strike the fly in embarrassment. Anyway, it was a number 12, if memory serves, and I stripped off some line and began false casting.

As soon as I lay the fly down I got a hit. Not expecting instant action, I missed it. The third cast produced another strike, and, more alert this time, I soon held a beautiful eight-inch cutthroat in my hand. I continued fishing, and in nothing flat I had enough for a good feed.

After we ate, while having coffee we noticed that Ruby was looking intently toward the lake, ears cocked, with a slight air of nervousness. Faint splashing noises, obviously produced by something large, drifted up to us. As we carried nothing more potent than a slingshot, we shared the mule's apprehension.

It was already dark, so we took a flashlight and, without lighting it, "injuned" down to the water's edge. After making sure that Greg wasn't blocking my escape route, I played the beam across the water to the source of the splashing noises. The narrow cone of light revealed a huge cow moose, its jaws draped with pond weeds, blindly staring back at us.

Greg's Eggs

She didn't seem to mind us in her home, and we were happy to discover our hostess was a vegetarian.

The sky was black and clear. There was no moon, but thousands of stars glittered like little diamonds. Without cloud cover, the air temperature dropped rapidly. Previous nights had hung in the low 60s, but that night was the first of a cooling trend and fell into the 40s with no delay. This is a guesstimate, as we hadn't a thermometer, but we didn't need one to tell us our sleeping bags were in the wrong camp.

We sat up late, feeding the fire, exchanging lies, postponing the inevitable, but finally ran out of bull stuffing and had to turn in. I piled more wood on the fire, laid out saddle pads for a mattress, and, rolled up in my manty, took on the appearance of a magnum burrito. I was cold immediately.

Staring up at a roof of stars usually delights me, but this night I was reminded of icicles. Turning my face to the fire, I thought of my Hollofil sleeping bag in the big tent at base camp. Then I thought of Scott and his pronouncement about wimps and mountain men, and resolved that if I lived, he would die.

At that point I almost dozed off, but Ruby foiled my attempt. Famous for her tuneful flatulence, her voice resembled a high-pitched trombone going down, and then back up, the musical scale. Just as I began drifting, she ripped one that went on for half a minute. If I hadn't been so damned miserable, I would have laughed.

Greg was doing no better. From time to time I'd hear him moan, then curse as he tried to roll up tighter in his manty. When I wasn't thrashing around, he was. Thus the night crept on, endlessly, in frigid punishment. I thanked the gods that at least we were dry.

Nothing lasts forever. The sun finally showed up to save us wretched pilgrims. Our gratitude knew no bounds. I had a popper of a fire going in about four seconds, give or take two, after rolling out of my manty. Considering how pitiful we'd felt for so long, we felt wonderful in a remarkably short time.

The next order of business was coffee, black as the inside of a bull and stout enough to float a horseshoe. After a couple of cups each, all doubt as to our

Greg's Eggs

survival vanished. Figuring our fates at least temporarily secure, we fixed our thoughts on some breakfast. I had rolled out first, renewed the fire and made coffee, so Greg stepped forward to tend to the cooking. Taking stock of our larder, he produced the following:

INGREDIENTS: Bacon, six slices; one medium-sized onion; six large eggs; small can of chopped green chili peppers; one large, baked potato (cold).

Dice the bacon strips into half inch squares and fry them medium crisp in a hot cast iron skillet. While the bacon is frying, slice the onion into eighths. Dump out two-thirds of the grease when the bacon is done and toss in the sliced onion. Now dice up your cold baked potato (left over from the previous night's supper), and toss the spuds in when the onion begins to soften. The bacon will finish getting done while the other proceedings take place.

When the taters get crispy, add the can of green chilies. When the peppers have been in the skillet for a minute or two, break your eggs in a pot or bowl and whip as you would for scrambling. Next, spread all the sauteed stuff evenly around the skillet and carefully pour the eggs in so as not to stir things up too much. In about another minute, when the eggs have stiffened some, scramble it all up, cook for one more minute, and Greg's Eggs are done. Dig in. Serves two.

By the way, from then on 'til the end of the school, Greg and I were known as the Manty Brothers.

Roast Wild Goose

For the waterfowler, the Canada goose is big game. And for those of us who bring the fruits of the hunt to the dinner table, the big honker is fare beyond compare.

I have a real soft spot in my heart for wild geese in general, and Canadas in particular. They mate for life, which is more than you can say for many humans, and their comings and goings in spring and fall make the seasons pass with natural grace. I've only taken a very few honkers during a lot of years of wild-fowling, and usually just as passing chances while duck hunting. If they weren't such good eating, I know I'd never have killed the first one.

You can rest easy in the knowledge that the Canada goose has never been so numerous or had as good a lifestyle as it has these days. One of the wariest game birds, it has never been a simple matter for the hunter to fill his limit of these geese. Add to that the fact that the Canada's nesting grounds are far enough north to be out of harm's way from the ravages of civilization, and that modern farming methods provide them with more winter food than ever before, and it becomes

obvious that we'll be hearing goose music for many seasons to come.

The following recipe is for roasting a young bird, under ten pounds dressed weight. Try this method on an old gander of fifteen or more pounds, however, and you'll not likely be able to shoot a hole in the gravy with a deer rifle. I've got other ways to deal with the older birds, which are revealed elsewhere in this book. So, here's Roast Wild Goose, done my way.

INGREDIENTS: One Canada honker, snow goose, or specklebelly, 6-10 pounds dressed weight; olive oil; garlic powder; coarse ground black pepper; piece of cheese cloth, 12 inches square.

Pick the goose thoroughly, then singe remaining pin feathers. Like ducks, young geese are best served medium rare, so I don't use stuffing but let the heat from the oven enter the body cavity to help the bird cook from the inside. Place goose breast-up in a covered turkey roaster, with enough water to cover the bottom pan to a depth of one-half inch. If there's room around the bird, put in a

Roast Wild Goose

few russet potatoes and onions to cook with it. Shake some garlic powder and black pepper on the breast. Next, saturate the cheese cloth with olive oil (if you don't like olive oil, use bacon grease or vegetable oil) and drape it over the bird, but be careful not to cover the hole in the body cavity (so heat can enter). The cheese cloth helps keep the bird moist and tender. Set oven at 325 degrees and cook the bird, covered in the roaster, for one hour.

After an hour, take the lid off the roaster and remove the cheese cloth. Then turn oven up to 400 degrees and let the bird cook uncovered for another half an hour to brown the skin. At the end of the combined hour and a half cooking time, make a cut in the breast along the keel bone. If red juices and pink flesh are what you see, she's done. If the meat is dark red, put the bird back in for another 15 minutes or so. If you want gravy, spoon the liquid fat off the drippings in the bottom of the roaster and discard. Set the roaster over a medium-hot stove element and add a little flour to the remaining drippings, stirring as it bubbles. That's all there is to it. A little salt to taste and you're in business.

Desert Rat Rabbit

Jackrabbit is not high on many people's lists of preferred cuisine. It has, however, graced many an economy-minded table over the years. During our westward expansion, the lowly Mr. Jack was consumed by the millions. Stuck on a stick and hung over the coals of a campfire, he was the wiener of the Plains.

In the days of the Nevada gold rush, prospectors poked into every nook and cranny of the territory, and when supplies ran low, jackrabbit often headlined the bill of fare. These old-timers were fondly known as "desert rats," and they are still around, looking for gold, silver, or anything of value. Maybe just peace of mind.

At one time I found myself living in Nevada outside the little town of Gardnerville. It was high desert country in the shadow of the Pine Nut Range. I was between jobs, living rent free in an old shack out on the sagebrush flats, and pretty much without funds. (Sort of a latter day desert rat.) About the only thing I had in abundance was jackrabbit, right out the back door.

Through much trial and error, I came up with a way to fix this stringy critter so it goes down easy. Here's how.

INGREDIENTS: One jackrabbit (preferably young); salt; vinegar; seasoned flour; oil or bacon grease.

1. Cut your rabbit up as you would chicken. Unless you've got a young one, under four pounds, throw the hind legs to your dog (bone the meat first, rabbit bones are brittle and could hurt your old buddy). The reason for this is that the hind legs of an adult jackrabbit are so gamey and strong that no amount of kitchen trickery will render them edible.

2. Wash the pieces and set them to soak overnight in a gallon of salt water with a half cup of vinegar.

3. Pour off the salt water and rinse. Cover with cold water and bring to a boil. Turn down heat and let simmer as slowly as possible for at least an hour.

4. Remove from water and let cool. Put some seasoned flour in a paper bag and drop in rabbit pieces and shake 'til flour covers them.

5. Heat a little bacon grease or other oil in a big iron skillet. Brown both sides of rabbit at high heat, reduce heat to low simmer, add a little water and cover skillet so rabbit will steam.

Should be done in about thirty minutes to an hour. Poke with a fork to check tenderness. Serve like fried chicken.

Glenn's Streamside Lunch

One bonus of living in Ennis, Montana was getting to fish with some of the top guides on the Madison River. This was back in the mid-seventies, before fishing pressure became so intense that the number of guided boats on the river resembled the Spanish Armada. Several of the guides were friends, so I was treated to some of the West's finest fly fishing without charge.

Thinking back on those trips, the best times were always with Glenn Law. He came to Montana from Missouri and took to the country like a native son. A powerful fly caster and oarsman, he was the complete guide; building his own boat, tying his own flies. But for all his expertise as a trout fisherman, his greatest talent was for showing his clients a good time. Even when the fishing was mediocre, Glenn's people enjoyed their day on the river.

One of the options Glenn offered was gourmet lunch prepared streamside. It wasn't the standard treatment, and cost extra, but as you'll see, was worth it and then some. But I'm getting ahead of myself, and I want to interject a fish story before we get to the recipe.

On days when Glenn wasn't booked, he'd usually take a busman's holiday and do a little fishing for his own pleasure. I recall one time in the spring of the year (I believe it was '79), before tourist season got underway. Glenn had an open slot in his schedule, and I managed to shirk whatever responsibilities I had that day. Naturally, there was no choice but to go fishing. This trip was a little different, however.

Ennis is a Mecca for hard-core fly fishermen, and possession of a spinning outfit is close to a hanging offense. On this occasion, Glenn and I dared to step totally out of character and brave the jeers of the fly-fishing fraternity. We'd been reminiscing about our Southeast and Midwest origins and lazy days of bait fishing on the lakes of our youth. In short order we talked each other into a re-enactment of bygone times.

In my endless array of defective sporting equipment was a much abused and many times previously owned jon boat. It was 12 feet long, aluminum, and only leaked about two gallons of water an hour. Without a motor and powered by oars, it was ideal for our radical plan. Into the back of my pickup it went, along with various tackle boxes, spinning rods, and

Glenn's Streamside Lunch

bait containers all borrowed from local meat fishermen.

Next stop was the neighborhood market to provision ourselves for the day. As it was an informal outing, we made do with a variety of junk food items for lunch and, of course, laid in a goodly supply of beer. Another quick stop for gas and we were gone.

Ennis Lake, previously known as Meadow Lake, was formed by the building of a small hydroelectric dam toward the head end of Bear Trap Canyon. Prior to the dam's construction, the area now submerged was formerly a low-lying meadow land famous for its yield of wild hay. Thus, the lake's original name. It has been silting in since its birth and its days of joy for waterskiers and fishermen are numbered. Its potential as a duck marsh, however, is outstanding. At any rate, this was our destination.

We put in at the McCallister access and began rowing for the main channel. In a short time we found ourselves surrounded by thick aquatic weeds growing right up to the surface. Oars were just the ticket, as an outboard propeller would have choked out in seconds. Even with oars, though, I had to stroke heroically to make headway.

It turned into a warm spring day, and with my strenuous rowing and Glenn's exhaustive barrage of instructions, we were ready for a beer before getting halfway to our anchor point. Knowing that the sun was over the yardarm somewhere in the world, we broke out the suds.

Finally winning free of the weeds, I was able to make good time again, and soon we drifted into the main channel of the river, standing off a short way from where it entered the lake. The current was mild but constant, so I made ready to drop anchor.

The anchor was well-suited to the boat. An empty gallon drywall mud bucket filled with cement, and a three-eighths-inch eyebolt cast in the center as a tie point for the rope. Ugly but economical, over the bow it went. As the bashed-up little craft slowly spun to face the current, we popped another beer apiece and cleared the decks for action.

Glenn's Streamside Lunch

Monofilament was stripped off reels, No. 6 bait hooks and splitshot attached accordingly. When all was in readiness, I produced the key ingredient — Milt Crooker's secret weapon, the jealously guarded killer bait. Trout roe cured in sugar, bagged up in little pieces of pantyhose to stay on the hook, but still release scent. I can feel you fly fishermen shudder and recoil, but I confess without regret that it was pure fun.

We caught no lunkers that day, but the small skillet trout were in good form, and as each beer was removed from the ice chest, its place was taken by a plump 10-inch rainbow. As I cleaned them before icing them down, any fresh roe I found was added to the curing jar. In this way we maintained our bait supply.

The day passed very agreeably. Lunch time came and we made short work of our chips and such, washed down with more bait-fisherman's brew. The boat leaked its traditional two gallons per hour, and we took turns bailing now and then with the plastic margarine tub brought along for that purpose. The fishing eventually slowed, but we had plenty by then.

The sun dropped behind the Gravelly Range about the time we finished the last beer, so we pulled on long-sleeve shirts and weighed anchor. Rowing back was a little crookeder than rowing out, but a lot more laughs. The weedbed was a bigger S.O.B. than ever, and by the time we beached her I was mostly sober. Driving home was safe enough, Montana traffic being what it is. All in all, it was a superb day.

So, next time you hear some purist spout that no real fly fisherman would ever touch bait and spinning gear, you can tell them that one of the finest fly guides who ever floated the Madison was once corrupted on a fine spring day. Glenn now lives in Florida, hunting tarpon and bonefish with a fly rod and writing about it for a living. Here's his recipe for streamside lunch, Madison River style.

Glenn's Streamside Lunch

INGREDIENTS: *Cooking trout (14" and under); pork chops or chicken (in case fishing is poor); white Mouton cadet, and plenty of it; cooking foil; campfire grill (one from an old refrigerator works great); black pepper; salt; garlic powder; big can paprika; butter; charcoal and lighter fluid; corn on the cob; French or sourdough bread; bagged salad (packed in cooler); salad dressing (in plastic bottle also packed in cooler).*

After tying up to the bank, find a place out of the wind for your fire. Clear away twigs, dry leaves or other burnables from the area. Gather up some round rocks for the fire ring, making sure they're dry. (Wet rocks can explode in the heat.) Fill the ring with dry branches or whatever else you have for kindling. Use small stuff. Lay your grill over the rocks and pile the charcoal right on top of it. Then cover the charcoal with more kindling. This is the key to a fast charcoal fire, ready to cook on much faster than usual. Douse the whole mess liberally with starter fluid and touch her off. While the fire burns down, prepare the main course.

Clean trout with head and tail on. Wrap in double layer of foil cut a little longer than the fish, add salt, pepper, a little butter plus a splash of wine over all. Seal ends of foil and set aside.

Take pork chops and chicken and sprinkle paprika over all surfaces until no more will stick. That's right, cover the meat completely with paprika. It serves to seal the meat as it cooks, and drips into the fire to make a fragrant smoke that flavors the meat as well. To quote Glenn, "Both Ed Curnow and Jack Cole claim to be the originators of this paprika technique. On separate occasions each has called the other a liar. Both are great cooks and great fishermen, but then all fishermen are liars. I have since resolved the dispute of the paprika tradition and am accepting it in the spirit in which it was handed down. I now claim the recipe as my own."

To prepare the corn, peel back the husk, but don't tear it off. Next, take a paper towel flat in your palm and lay the ear of corn in your hand. Twist back and forth and watch the silk come off. Now, place a pat or two of butter under husk and pull it back up. Splash some wine over the husks and

Glenn's Streamside Lunch

wrap the ears in foil. Set aside. Slice bread almost through, apply butter and garlic powder between slices and wrap in double foil. Set aside.

By now the coals are most likely ready, so slide them off the grill and into the fire pit. Heavy leather gloves are handy if you have them. Take a stick and scatter the coals evenly, and replace grill about eight inches over the fire. Now lay your corn around the perimeter of the bed of coals where it's hottest. The fish go in the cooler part of the fire against the rocks.

Up on the grill put the meat over the coals and your bread to one side. Keep your eye on the meat so that it drips and smokes but doesn't burn. Turn the bread back and forth every couple of minutes.

Down in the pit, spin the corn a quarter turn every five minutes. The fish will take five to seven minutes a side, depending on size. It's done when the tail sticks to the foil. Use your heavy gloves and a pair of pliers to check.

Take your bagged salad out of the cooler now. Fresh spinach is a good green as it is durable and travels well. You can dump your bottled dressing right in the bag with the salad and shake it up.

Glenn recommends taking heavy plastic plates and metal flatware. Show the professional touch with a few "creature comforts." It makes a big difference in the way the meal is received. So that's it. Dig in and enjoy!

Afterwards, pitch your grill into the river to cool. Then put it in a big plastic bag to keep soot off your outfit. Put plates and utensils in plastic bags, too, for home cleaning. Glenn says, "There's nothing enjoyable, romantic or entertaining about doing streamside dishes; you'll just have to do them again at home anyway."

One final word concerning the paprika technique. Inasmuch as Glenn inherited the tradition from Cole and/or Curnow, and afterwards claimed the recipe as his own, I can do no less than carry on that fine tradition. I accept the recipe with grateful compliments, and henceforth shall credit myself as its originator. Much obliged, Glenn.

Tom's Clam Sauce Spaghetti

Coming by this recipe was a real pleasure. After many seasons in the Sierras and northern Rockies, I finally got to make a trip to the North Cascades. What country! Shark's tooth peaks, ragged ridges, glacial streams, and big timber, deep and black with red-gold maples scattered throughout. Little valleys with log cabins and pole corrals, horses belly deep in golden grass. Good medicine.

The occasion was a deer hunt in Washington state, with Tom McDonald of Seattle. I met Tom when he got together with a lady friend of my wife and me. We buddied up right away.

Tom has a little piece of property on the Methow River, in the shadow of the Pasayten Wilderness. We made our deer camp there, and a finer setting would be hard to come by. The parcel runs right down to the water — sandy soil, screening willows and towering cottonwoods make it a camper's dream come true. And it's deer country.

With a father of Scottish descent and an Italian mother, Tom is an interesting combination. His dark eyes and hair show the Mediterranean blood combined with the hard, chiseled features of the highlander. From his mom he learned to love pasta, and how to cook it. Clam sauce spaghetti may seem a little exotic for a mountain deer camp, but it was just the right fuel for rambling the heights on foot. Before the recipe, though, let's have the story.

On this hunt, Tom and I sort of guided each other. Tom knew the country but was not a hunter — deer or otherwise. I'd never set foot in the territory but had a little savvy concerning how to gather venison chops. Pooling our knowledge seemed to be a good plan.

The first night in camp was all you could want. Not a cloud or a breath of wind; so nice we never pitched our tent. After a good solid supper and a couple of hours of hot tea and fire gazing, we rolled out our bags and crawled in. A little time spent counting shooting stars was all I needed to slip off. We slept as only those under no roof can sleep.

Morning found us dusted with a rime of frost. The night had been below freezing, but as the sun rose so did the temperature. We breakfasted on cooked cereal, cheese, and hot tea, grabbed our rifles and

Tom's Clam Sauce Spaghetti

forded the river. It was very low that late in the fall, and stepping stones provided us a dry crossing. Climbing the cutbank, we entered the timber.

According to Tom, both whitetails and mule deer were commonly seen on this side of the river. It consisted of a level forest floor running back from the water a hundred yards or so before climbing gradually to rugged shoulders below the peaks. The big trees and a grassy understory looked like game country to me.

An old logging road paralleled the river and, filled with fallen pine needles from many seasons, made for noiseless walking. We eased along without a sound, and the glory of the morning was like a tonic. Wherever a trickle crossed the road to join the river, damp earth showed deer tracks.

That morning was the season opener for the area, and we knew that other hunters would be out and about. Even so, the crashing report of a deer rifle up ahead caused us both to jump. The shot came from close by, and I wondered if it had connected. Before the

thought cooled in my head, I heard thundering hooves on the trail. Tom heard them too, and we had just enough time to throw each other a quizzical glance before the buck came into view.

It was a young, forkhorn mulie, and he was packing the mail. He saw us about the time we saw him, and for an instant I thought I'd be run down. Tom and I stepped off the trail to the right, the buck swung wide to the left. I was out of position to shoot, but Tom let fly a round as the deer streaked past.

To make a long story short, the deer escaped unharmed. We hunted the rest of the day. If I recall correctly, I killed a spruce grouse with my .22 pistol. We spit cooked the grouse and shared it at lunch time. Evening saw us coming across the river with heavy boots, happy to see camp.

After the fire was going and the tea water on, Tom declared it was time for clam sauce spaghetti. There was no argument from me, so he commenced preparations. Here, then, is Tom's Clam Sauce Spaghetti.

Tom's Clam Sauce Spaghetti

INGREDIENTS: *6-ounce can of minced clams; 1 garlic clove, minced; 1/4 stick butter; 2 tablespoons parsley flakes; 1/2 lb. uncooked spaghetti; 2 table-spoons olive oil; 2 quarts water.*

Boil the water and add olive oil, then the spaghetti. If you're camped at high altitude, remember that water takes longer to boil (has to do with less atmospheric pressure), so allow plenty of time.

While the spaghetti cooks, melt the butter in a skillet. When the water begins to bubble nicely, add the garlic and parsley flakes. After three or four minutes, stirring the while, dump in the clams with the liquid that comes in the can. Simmer the combined ingredients for another couple of minutes, then check your spaghetti. When you can throw a single strand against a flat surface and it sticks, then it's done. (The tailgate of your truck will do just fine as a target.)

Next, pour off the spaghetti water and slosh a little fresh water over the noodles to rinse off the starch. Pour the clam sauce hot from the skillet over the spaghetti. Plumb simple. Serves two hungry folks.

Rock Bass on the Beach

What do you think of when someone mentions the Baja Peninsula of Mexico? The beach is first in most folks' minds, and that's where we headed in the spring of '72. (Now, I know this is slanted to be a mountain cookbook, but this is a good story and a good recipe, so please indulge me. Besides, we could see desert mountains from our camp.)

It was the shank of a long winter and I was living on the south shore of Lake Tahoe, loading chairs at a ski area. The young lady I was paying attention to at the time recommended that we pool our resources with another couple and drive right out of winter and into the sun and sand of Old Mexico. I agreed.

We decided on the west coast of the Sea of Cortez, or Gulf of California — two names for the same body of water, take your pick. More specifically, we were headed for a town called San Felipe, at the northern end of the Baja Peninsula. The place sort of grew up around American fishing camps and local commercial operations run by Mexican fishermen. It sounded good to a bunch of snow-burned mountain kids. Our gear went in the bed of my friend's pickup, the four of us crammed in the cab, and south we went.

Highway 395 runs down the eastern side of the Sierra Nevada Range, right past the tallest peaks of the High Sierras. That was our road out of winter, and the mountain scenery alone was worth the drive. We rubbernecked along like farmers in town.

A friend of our travelling companions lived in Los Angeles, so we laid up there the first night. We crossed over next morning at Calexio. Still stateside, I got to feeling funny while riding in the back of the truck. As we neared the border, I lost my breakfast right over the side of the pickup bed. Great! I thought, not even in Mexico and sick already. But as it turned out, that was my only ill moment on the entire expedition.

If you've ever been to Mexico, you may have noticed how abruptly things seem to change. Cross the border and the country is immediately dry, the roads are rougher, and the cops are fatter. Buzzards sit on telephone poles. Stuff like that. But all the differences aren't necessarily bad ones. Things slow down quite a bit. And, most times, slower is okay by me. The pace of the Baja country suits me fine.

Rock Bass on the Beach

The rest of the drive was as beautiful as the first part. It had rained, as it does on rare occasions in the desert, and all the cactus, and every other thing that could make a flower, was blooming. We passed houses that looked to be made of cardboard, and I thought that with no more rain than they got there, maybe a cardboard house worked just fine. We made San Felipe late in the afternoon.

We found a hotel that let us camp on their beach for a couple of bucks, so we picked a spot, fixed some supper, and then went beach combing. We dug some clams, but they were so small we put them back. They didn't seem to mind. When it got dark, we shook our bags out and turned in.

All agreed next morning to hunt a rangier stretch of beach, one without use fees. While breakfast was fixing, I went on a little recon stroll around the hotel grounds. As I circled back downwind, the breeze brought a pleasing whiff from the breakfast fire, so I turned toward camp.

After consuming a satisfying bait of grub, which contained surprisingly little sand, we broke camp and moved on.

While we rode along, it became apparent that this was a retirement haven for American seniors. We were continually passed by stripped-down VW bugs lustily driven by little, nut brown, scantily clad oldsters, uniformly topped by Panama hats.

The beach was endless and empty, so when a sandy two-track offered a way down to the water, we took it. After poking around for a few minutes, we found a low ridge that formed a dished out spot in the lee of the wind, and made our new camp.

The rest of the day was spent exploring the territory. As far as I could look up and down the beach, there was no one. We shared the world we could see with one lonesome trawler, far out on the horizon. The sun drowned out in the Pacific. At my back, the moon popped up like a flashing bobber from the Gulf.

Rock Bass on the Beach

I rolled out next morning to the sight of the finest sunrise of my life. Quite a statement, but even now, across the years, nothing has matched it. A red-orange ball of fire rising out of the water to fight its way up through scrapings of gun-metal clouds.

This was to be a day of fishing, so we headed into San Felipe to outfit ourselves. We needed bait, beer, and air for our rubber raft. The girls wanted to hit the shops. Arriving in town, we dispersed at once. First order of business was a stop at the bait shop. Chopped mackerel, we were told, was a good all-purpose offering, so we stocked up. Next we aired up the raft at a filling station and grabbed some beer.

Suitably equipped, Chris and the girls and I headed for a spot close to town that the bait shop guy had recommended. Our timing was right. The tide was just coming in. The northern end of the Sea of Cortez is so narrow that the tide comes up at an amazing rate. Chris and I simply carried the raft out onto the flats and set it down. Having no anchor, we tied the painter to a rock and waited. The girls spread their towels above the high tide line and plopped down for some rays.

The wait was a short one. Sea water came bubbling across the tide flats, pushing a little head of foam along its front. It washed across our feet and rushed on northward. We gaped at each other and burst out laughing. It was like standing in a giant, rapidly filling bath tub, waiting for your rubber ducky to float. The rising water lifted the raft, and when the water was thigh deep we hopped in.

Rigging up quickly, we baited with malodorous chunks of mackerel and heaved out from opposite ends of the raft. This was an old navy survival job, which was rated for six shipwrecked mariners. It accommodated two laid back bait fishermen in regal comfort. We hunkered down like overfed dogs and awaited further developments.

The morning was another jewel. A fresh, salty breeze came along with the tide, and the sky was powder

Rock Bass on the Beach

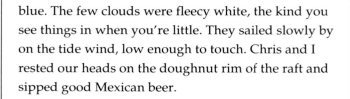

blue. The few clouds were fleecy white, the kind you see things in when you're little. They sailed slowly by on the tide wind, low enough to touch. Chris and I rested our heads on the doughnut rim of the raft and sipped good Mexican beer.

After driving down from six feet of snow three days before, this was simply unbelievable. As we bobbed in the gentle chop, squadrons of brown pelicans flew over in formation, like B-17s crossing the English Channel. We lay back in the raft like castaway idiots, grinning 'til our faces hurt. I was about to comment to Chris on the surreal nature of our situation when his rod tip went over the side.

I yelled what everybody does when the fish is on someone else's line. "Get your tip up!" Chris laughed and made guttural noises, the rod bucking wildly. This was a sure enough fish, I thought — maybe a barracuda or a little hammerhead. I really hoped it was something more edible, such as a flounder.

My friend continued to giggle maniacally, as he always did with a fish on. The line cut the water, closer and closer to the raft. "I can see him!" Chris yelled, and with a manly backward lunge, drew his prize from the Gulf. Arching through the air, to dance venomously only inches above my laps was a mad-as-hell, two-foot sting ray, its barbed tail whipping and cracking over my tender parts.

Chris held the rod as high as he could, and I'm sure it was only seconds that the angry little creature lashed wickedly within a whisper of my bare legs. But I know that it carved five years off my life and seemed to go on forever. "Over the side! Over the side!" No doubt, my screams were heard south of the Panama Canal. Two weeks (at least) later, Chris managed to bounce his catch back into the water.

By then I was sitting in a puddle. Probably it was bilge. I'm sure it was the color of the raft that made it look yellow. In a move that would shame the local toughs, I whipped out my pocket knife and cut the line. Chris didn't argue.

Rock Bass on the Beach

After a calming interval and a couple more beers, we resumed fishing. I got the next hit, and after a quick but exacting check, brought in a fat little fish locally referred to as a rock bass. It was about the size and shape of a fresh water rock bass, or red-eye. We must have been in the path of a school, for in no time we had a sackful, each one a clone of the next. When we had collected enough for a good feed, we weighed anchor and paddled for shore.

Here, then, is Rock Bass on the Beach.

INGREDIENTS: Two or three eight-inch rock bass per person (any panfish will do — bluegill, perch, crappie, and so on).

Seasoned flour or cornmeal, your choice; 1/2 teaspoon crushed red pepper; peanut oil.

Heat oil in iron skillet over your campfire (or range, if you're at home on the range). When the oil is good and hot, but not quite smoking, put in the crushed pepper and stir gently every now and then for five minutes. This will spice the oil and flavor the fish. Roll the fish in flour or cornmeal and place in skillet. Oil should cover the fish halfway. Depending on size of fish and temperature of oil, seven to ten minutes a side should be about right. Serve with fried potatoes and whatever else you like to have with fish. It's a simple recipe that provides a little snap to the flavor of fish. Eat hearty.

Sloan's Smoked Salmon

If you're like most of the rest of us, you probably don't often find yourself in the position of having caught too many fish. Not legally, anyway. It happened to me once, though, and we had to rig a make-shift smoker to preserve our catch. Here's how it happened.

Frank Sloan, an old fishing buddy from Texas, had decided to ride up to Montana with me on a land scouting trip. I was looking for a couple of acres to build a cabin on and I thought the Big Sky country was the place for me. We loaded our camping and fishing outfit into my pickup and left Lake Tahoe around the first of September, 1974.

Crossing northern Nevada was a hot, dry run. We tried a little rabbit and partridge hunting along the way, but with little success. Without a gun dog, it was a crapshoot at best. We'd made a vow to each other to conserve cash by eating meat only when we got it from the wild, so we discovered that we had become involuntary vegetarians in a short time.

Poking along in no particular hurry, we crossed over into Idaho a couple of days later. Mile after mile of potato country, flat and shapeless, like west Texas hauled up north. The land began to change, and when we hit Boise it was beginning to look like the Northwest. The sight of tall pines was heaven to my eyes.

We stopped at a sporting goods store to ask about fishing. The saleslady told us to head for Little Camas Reservoir because the kokanee salmon were over-populated there. They were maturing and spawning at about ten or eleven inches in length when the average adult should run sixteen to eighteen inches. This was due to overcrowding, so the Idaho Game and Fish Department had opened a special snagging season to try to thin out the ranks. We would be allowed 25 fish apiece.

After buying non-resident permits and getting directions, we drove to the South Boise River, which feeds the reservoir. The salmon were supposedly spawning in huge concentrations, so we drove the road beside the stream and looked for red fish. Kokanee turn bright red when spawning (they're a smaller cousin to the sockeye of Alaskan waters), and we tried to spot them in the river.

Sloan's Smoked Salmon

Miles went by with no sign of a fin, and we thought we'd been sent on another wild fish chase. When we were on the brink of hanging it up, rounding one more curve turned up what we were looking for — a lovely little falls, dropping some fifteen feet, with an emerald pool at the bottom. This hole was about 50 feet in diameter, and just under the surface it was living red. The salmon were jammed in like Tokyo office workers on a commuter train. A sheep dog could have crossed the river on the fishes' backs.

Frank looked at the pool and then at me. He grinned and made for the back of the truck and his fishing gear. I was right behind him, and soon we were rigged with big treble hooks, lashing the water without mercy. It took just over an hour to limit out.

A little ways upstream, along the river bank, was a beautiful sandy campsite surrounded by willows and spruce. We pulled in, and while Frank cleaned fish, I built a fire. We'd had no meat for three days and were craving a feast of fine, pink salmon flesh. When the fire was strong enough to take care of itself, I helped Frank with the rest of the cleaning.

Two skillets on the camp grill, filled with hissing, popping fish, is a sight to inspire a starving camper. Frank tended his pan and I mine, and a little later we lay in the sand like two gorged lions after consuming a water buffalo. Memory tells me we downed seven fish each, plus some fried roe. The effect of such a protein overdose, especially after such a hiatus from meat, was profound. Suffice to say that there was enough methane in the air around our camp that night to burn the Hindenberg all over again.

There was still a pile of salmon to deal with, and since we were truck camping without refrigeration, preservation was a challenge. Frank came up with the idea to build a smoker and do the fish Indian style. We had a piece of plastic sheeting about eight feet square, so we tied some little limbs into a tepee frame and made a smoke tent. And here's Frank Sloan's recipe for smoked salmon.

Sloan's Smoked Salmon

INGREDIENTS: Three green limbs about 1 1/2 inches in diameter and six feet long.

One piece of sheet plastic, eight to ten feet square.

Twenty feet of binder twine or light-weight cord.

Fifteen or twenty green branches, 1/2 inch diameter by two feet long.

Big mess of fish (any kind, if they're not much longer than a foot) cleaned with head and tail on.

Form a tripod with your long sticks by tying the tops together tepee style. Then tie three of the shorter sticks horizontally from pole to pole, about halfway up from the ground, to make a framework for your fish rack. Now lay the remaining sticks across this frame about an inch and a half apart to put the fish on. Finally, wrap the plastic snugly around this structure, leaving a tiny draw hole at the top to act as a chimney. Fold the plastic up from the ground a couple of feet so as not to burn it, and build your fire.

Get a good bed of coals before lowering the plastic again. As for the fish, split them down the backbone and open them out, butterfly fashion. Salt them a little, if you like, and lay them flesh side down on the rack. To make smoke, put wet hardwood chips on your bed of coals. (Lacking wet wood chips, we used green willow boughs. It worked, but I'd rather have hardwood.) Now and then you'll have to add a dry stick to the fire so the coals stay strong, but not too much or you'll cook your fish.

Keep this up for eight or ten hours and your fish will be done. It's a good excuse to stand around and drink beer all day. The fish should keep a week or two, depending on how dry you smoke 'em. I don't know exactly how long they'll keep because we ate ours up in about three days.

Cherry Lake Hot Spiced Tea

This recipe is for a refreshing potion from my wife's bag of camp kitchen tricks. She first served it to me on our honeymoon, a pack trip to Cherry Lake, at the north end of Montana's Madison Range. It's just the thing when you want a hot drink back in the hills but are maybe tired of coffee.

Shirley and I had been married going on two years before we ever got around to a honeymoon. A friend had sent us to a resort for one night in a cabin as a wedding present, and due to our work commitments, that's as close to a honeymoon as we got for a while. So, when the chance came for us both to take a week off together, we caught the horses and readied our gear.

What we didn't have was a pack mule, so I borrowed one from an old hunting pal, Robin Shipman. (He shows up in a couple other places in this book.) He was happy to let us have Josephine for a week. Robin and I ran our stock together a good part of the time, so all the critters were well acquainted. They piled in the four-horse trailer like a bunch of eager kids, and we drove off down the road in a hail o' hen shit.

This would be my first ride in to Cherry Lake and Shirley's first time horseback in many years. I wanted to make a short trip in so as not to sore her up too bad. My trusty Forest Service map said seven miles from the trailhead to the lake. She figured she could handle that, so we drove down into Bear Trap Canyon to the head of the Cherry Creek trail and packed up. It was a gorgeous July morning, and as I swung up on the mare and pointed her up the trail, I felt like the king of the world.

You may have guessed by now that I got us lost, and seven miles turned into twelve. When dark forced us to stop and make camp, my tender bride was so stove up I had to peel her off her mount like old house paint. She had stopped speaking to me about three miles back. The trouble had begun with an old sun bleached wooden trail marker that showed the cutoff to Cherry Lake from the main trail. The sign was so weathered and the cutoff so grown up that I'd ridden right past it. It took nearly three miles of wrong-way travel for me to get un-flummoxed. That added six

Cherry Lake Hot Spiced Tea

miles to the trip, and my poor red-headed partner felt every step of it.

To add insult to injury, when I did get us headed right, I promptly got myself bucked off. We were crossing a little meadow when the lead rope to the pack mule's halter got under my mare's tail. Her instant reaction was to clamp down on it. The more I tried to pull it loose, the more agitated she became. Finally, with me twisted way around in the saddle, totally off balance, she bogged her head and crow hopped, her front legs locked stiff in front of her. My reaction was to describe a short, smooth arc over her bent neck and come to rest in the middle of the trail in front of her. Flat on my back in a cloud of settling dust, I moved first one part of my body and then another. Everything still worked, so I got up. My .357 magnum handgun lay in the dirt. I picked it up, blew the dust off, and holstered it. Shirley's only comment was that I was lucky not to have a bullet through both hams.

Of course, Josephine took this opportunity to switch ends and head for the trailer. I bailed on the mare and chased her down. Ten minutes later we were underway again.

As mentioned earlier, it got dark on us before we found Cherry Lake, so we camped at a little snow-melt pond that had grass around it for the stock. While Shirley nursed her aching legs and seat, I pitched the tent and built a fire. After a quick supper, we turned in.

The next day dawned in mountain glory. The sky was clear, the breeze was light, and we both felt better. The pond was full of little frogs, and my golden retriever, who'd accompanied us, was busy catching them in the water. When he captured a frog, he'd bring it out to the bank and spit it out. He did this over and over — a regular catch and release dog — and I laughed 'til I could barely get my air. We rode on to the lake that afternoon.

Cherry Lake Hot Spiced Tea

Except for a little bear scare, the rest of the week was outstanding. As we trailed along to the lake that second afternoon, I pointed out some bear droppings on the trail. Shirley immediately became nervous, despite my efforts to minimize the chances of an encounter. I'd brought along a short-barreled 12 gauge shotgun for emergencies, and she was within ten feet of it for the rest of the trip.

But Mr. Bear never showed, and our stay was blessed with perfect weather. The cutthroat trout in Cherry Lake were typically cooperative, and our little honeymoon was a smashing success. Each night, beside the campfire, we toasted the mountain with hot spiced tea. Here's how Shirley makes it.

INGREDIENTS: 1 1/4 cups Tang™ Instant Breakfast Drink; 1/2 cup sugar; 1/3 cup instant tea; 1/2 teaspoon cinnamon; 1/4 teaspoon ground cloves.

Combine all the ingredients and store them in a zip-lock plastic bag. For one serving, place one well-rounded teaspoon of mix in a cup, fill with hot water, and stir until dissolved. Use more or less mix per serving, depending on how strong you like your tea.

Blue Paradise Punch

Here's another beverage born on a Montana pack trip. I'll include a disclaimer to the effect that this is powerful stuff to be used sparingly. Be especially sparing at high altitude, as the toll taken by alcohol increases the higher you climb. Having said that, I'll tell the story of its birth.

For two years I lived in a little cabin on a woman's ranch in southwest Montana. Juanita Stalcup was the most gracious of landladies, and for doing a few easy chores around her place I got the cabin rent-free. Her son, Ross, was a good friend, and every chance we got we were horseback in the hills.

One early September, Ross and I planned a pack trip into the Hilgarde Basin of the Madison Range, for a little trout fishing and camp loafing. The Hilgarde is a short section of the Madison Range that is extremely rugged, looking much like the Swiss Alps. They lie close to the northern border of Yellowstone National Park, and pretty country it is.

Our destination was Blue Paradise Lake, one of a number of small alpine lakes in the basin. Most of these lakes hold trout, and all are beautiful. We had a week to roam around and look them over.

Unloading the horses above the Beaver Creek campground, we began the ten-mile ride to the lake. A cold rain began falling soon after we started in, and by the time we reached the lake we were soaked and miserable. September usually provides some nasty weather in the mountains and we were getting a good dose of it now. While Ross hunted up dry wood, I broke down the sodden packs. In another hour we had the tent pitched and our gear covered with a tarp. About sundown the rain quit, and we were treated to a terrific sunset. Exhausted from the cold, wet ride, we turned in right after supper.

Dawn lit up a glistening alpine world, rain-wet rocks steaming in the sun. That was the way the rest of the trip went — cold nights and warm, golden days. Ross and I fished and rode the country, cooked and ate, and lounged around camp. We'd packed some books, as we were both big readers, and during the midday lull in fishing we'd lay up by the fire and get lost in a potboiler.

One of the items that came up the trail with us was a quart bottle of Jose Cuervo Gold Tequila. The third day of our trip, with the morning sun climbing toward

Blue Paradise Punch

noon, Ross broke out the jug and a jar of Tang. Then he packed a bucket of cold water up from the lake and built a batch of punch. We read our books and drank our punch, and all was right with the world.

I must have dozed off, 'cause next thing I knew the sun was straight up and Ross was sitting with his back against a pine tree, out cold as a wedge. Not wanting to spend the day looking at my partner's comatose body, I got up and tried my legs. Ross had sampled quite a bit more punch than I, and its effects hadn't gotten to me quite as thoroughly. Feeling just fine, in fact, I decided a ride up to Expedition Pass was in order. The mare must have thought so too, and seemed ready as I saddled her. She was chugging up the trail before my foot found the offside stirrup.

How do I describe the feeling of sitting a powerful, eager saddle horse and drifting through some of the most spectacular country on this planet? Ya gotta be there! This particular mare was a thoroughbred/quarter horse cross, with smooth gaits and good stride. In just a little bit we could see the top of the pass.

Then, a movement caught my eye. A lone horseman, coming up the trail from Expedition Lakes, on the east side of the pass. We topped out on the divide at the same time.

He rode a little palomino gelding, and from the look of them they'd come a good piece. The horse was pretty well rode down, and dropped his head as soon as his rider drew rein. The man in the saddle was hatless, his long hair held back by a twisted bandanna. That he'd spent a good many days in the open showed on his face and hands. As I rode near, he revealed white teeth inside a big smile.

"Aha, I see you 'av zee horse for zee Montana!"

A Frenchman! And complimenting me on my good mountain horse. I asked him where he rode from. Montreal to Vancouver, with a dip down into the United States for some sightseeing in the American Rockies.

It was my turn to compliment him on the grand scale of his ride. But now he told me he was turned around and wondered if I knew the way to the Beaver Creek trail. I told him his luck was changing for the better

Blue Paradise Punch

because we could see it from where we sat our mounts on the heights. The trail ran down the hillside below us, a good mile distant, but was easily spotted in the clear mountain air. He smiled again and thanked me.

Next he turned in the saddle and dug into his cantle roll, producing a pint bottle of Jim Beam, which he politely offered, once he had removed its cap. We sat our horses head to tail, so with an easy reach and a nod of thanks, I took a healthy pull and passed it back. He seemed pleased, and without wiping the neck, took a good slug himself. Digging into his kit once more, he came up with a pack of Camel straights and shook one out at me. Not much of a smoker, I made an exception. As we smoked and chatted, I thought that it must have been like this a hundred and fifty years back when free trappers met on the trail and shared a drink, a smoke, and exchanged mountain news.

Finishing our cigarettes, we shook hands and rode our separate trails — his to Vancouver, mine to camp. Ross was up and grumpy, his usual size seven head puffed up to an eight and a half. That punch had punch! And here's how it's made.

INGREDIENTS: 1 quart bottle of Jose Cuervo Gold Tequila; 1 large jar of Tang™; 1/2 gallon cold water from Blue Paradise Lake.

Mix the ingredients in a bucket and drink it up. Couldn't be easier. But watch your step, partner.

P.S. You don't have to get your water from Blue Paradise Lake, but your punch won't be near as good if you don't.

Saddle of Elk, Larded and Barded

Elk meat is considered by many to be the finest of wild game flesh, and elk hunting to be one of the most physically demanding field sports one can pursue. I'll back those opinions from first-hand experience, but I don't experience elk hunting as sport. It's more like work. And, like work, it can be fun or it can be miserable, or both.

But there's nothing miserable about this recipe, for the saddle is the prime cut of the elk, roughly the equivalent of standing rib roast of beef, without the fat. The larding and barding process keeps the meat moist and succulent, and no cut of beef can compare.

It's true that hunting elk can be a grueling experience, and I've never been colder or more exhausted than while chasing these great deer. But my fondest memory of past elk hunts involved no great stress or discomfort. This hunt went the way all hunts should go, but few do.

None of my hunting buddies could get away that weekend, so I caught the mare and hauled her to the trailhead alone. Camp was already set up and well stocked, sleeping bags hung from the tent's ridge pole, and plenty of good chuck filled the pack boxes. The seven-mile ride clicked by quick and easy, and soon the mare had her snout in a pile of hay and pellets while I stirred a skillet of beans. I turned in early.

Sometime in the black hour before dawn I heard voices outside the tent. It sounded like horsemen riding by and talking. I poked my head outside the front flap, but saw nothing against the white carpet of snow. Must have dreamed it, I thought, but at least I was up and moving.

A cold biscuit and a cup of creek water don't do much to warm a body's innards, and the 10 degree air got through my clothes before the saddle was on the mare. By the time we topped out on the divide between Bear Creek and Muddy Basin, dawn was coming on and I was chilled to the core. I tied the mare and took a stand where I could watch a good chunk of the meadow below me, but after an hour I'd had it. Visions of a blackened coffeepot hopping around on top of a glowing sheepherder stove inside

Saddle of Elk, Larded and Barded

the cozy wall tent hounded my brain, so I clambered up on the mare like a knight in frozen armor and headed down my backtrail.

And then I wasn't cold anymore because crossing the tracks my mare had left on the way in were the splayed prints of a single elk. They hadn't been there when we came in earlier, I was sure of that. And I knew that more often than not an elk traveling alone would be a bull. I turned the mare onto the new trail and followed it down off the divide into Muddy Basin.

When the timber got too thick for my horse to pass through, I tied her again and took the track on foot. The elk had bedded once and gotten up, meandering on in no particular direction. The bed was still warm when I came up on it. He was close now, and I studied the tracks with hypnotic intensity. They led into a small clearing, looking fresher with each step. A little corn snow had been falling, but there was almost none in the freshest prints. I knew I was

getting very close to the elk, and when I looked up, there he stood, sixty yards distant.

He faced away at a quartering angle, grazing unconcernedly, pawing at the snow like an old pasture bull. His tawny coat and chocolate mane were beautiful, and he was as big as a barn. There was no wind, and he hadn't spotted me.

With six points on a side, he was the first big bull I'd been close to. I flicked the safety off as I dropped to one knee. The .270 did its work cleanly. A few minutes later, when I stood beside him, I was overwhelmed. He was big, and we sure did need the meat at home. I thanked him in my heart for giving himself up to me and my family. At that moment I felt tied to the oldest and deepest relationship man can experience with nature.

We brought the mules in a couple days later to pack him out, and I can still see his rack rocking back and forth on top of one of the packsaddles as clear as a Kodak.

Saddle of Elk, Larded and Barded

A few weeks later, I served the saddle roast at a dinner for close friends. I fixed it like this.

INGREDIENTS: One saddle of elk (center cut from the back — works with deer and antelope as well); 1/4 cup pork fat diced into quarter-inch cubes; 2 large garlic cloves sliced into slivers; half dozen slices of lean bacon; coarse-ground black pepper.

Trim all fat and sinew off roast. Pierce meat randomly with a steak knife and push a sliver of garlic down into the puncture. Follow it with a chunk of the diced pork. This is the larding process (it flavors the meat and keeps it moist). Place your punctures one and a half inches apart over the entire roast.

Now for the barding. Drape bacon slices over the top of the roast, pinning them down with toothpicks. This keeps the surface moist. Sprinkle black pepper over all. This cut will weigh five to six pounds, so set your oven at 350 degrees and cook about 1 1/2 hours. Serve medium rare, as most game is dry if well done. Serves six.

Antelope Fillet

This is another very simple recipe. If you can grill a hamburger, you can do justice to an antelope fillet. Timing is the trick because overcooking game is a crime against nature.

My first try at antelope hunting was a comedy of errors. It was my second year in Montana and I was between carpenter jobs and short on cash and meat both. I didn't even own a deer rifle at the time, so I borrowed one from a friend. He wasn't much of a hunter, and the gun he loaned me proved it. It was a much neglected '94 Winchester 30-30. The extractor was broken, so each time it was fired, the shooter was obliged to knock out the empty case with a ramrod, or else dig it out with a pocket knife. This effectively turned a six-shot repeater into a single-shot rifle that shot about as slow as a black powder muzzleloader .

There was a small bunch of pronghorn living in a little draw up behind my place, so I took my borrowed one-shooter and walked a loop around and above the draw so as to come at the antelope from above. On the way up I took a longish shot at a mule deer and missed. I was still nearly a mile from where I expected to find my game and I didn't expect the shot would spook them. It didn't.

Sure enough, they were right where they belonged, about thirty head, grazing contentedly like so many Borden cows. I checked the wind, which was in my favor, visually picked a route that offered the most cover, and commenced my stalk. The timber got thin and then petered out altogether. When there was nothing left to hide behind, I got down on my belly and did the G.I. knees-and-elbows crawl. This was especially fun, due to the two inches of snow and freezing mud on the ground. But, as I said before, I was out of meat.

The antelope were still two hundred yards out when an old doe spotted me. She didn't know just what I was, but she knew a predator when she saw one. Stomping back and forth, showing alarm, she soon had the whole outfit nervous. They were way out of range of my defective carbine and they had me cold.

Antelope Fillet

If you've read anything about antelope, you probably are aware of their curiosity and how the oldtimers used to "flag 'em in," waving bandannas or shirts in the air. The inquisitive antelope, seeing something so strange in their quiet world, are drawn into range as if on a string. At least that's how the articles in the outdoor magazines made it sound. Having nothing to lose, I decided to give it a try.

I had no bandanna and wasn't about to take off my shirt in the 35°-degree air. Besides, it was wet. So, I just sat up on my haunches and rocked back and forth, reeling like a drunk. Fully expecting the band of pronghorn to cut and run, I was surprised to see the old doe come tap dancing toward me. She came twenty yards and stopped, so I stopped too. When she looked like she might turn back, I started my weird act again, and again she came a little closer. Over the course of the next hour, I got her to come within one hundred yards, and the bunch came with her.

At about eighty yards, I drew a bead on the brisket of a tasty looking little buck that was facing me. The hammer fell with a sickening "clack," and then I remembered the missed shot at the deer. I worked the lever to bring up a fresh round but was stymied by the broken extractor. My nerves were shot as I reached for my knife. The antelope looked nervous as well, but they waited patiently as I dug out the spent case and chambered a fresh round. The same buck still stood head on. He spun at the shot and was down within ten yards.

Antelope don't get very big, and a field dressed buck is an easy shoulder carry. But their hollow hair comes out quicker than a shedding cat's fur, and by the time I made the truck it was a good guess as to which of us was wearing more of it. But I had a good bait of meat now and my wool shirt would brush out. I was happy.

The fillet is the choice cut on the carcass and comes from the backstrap or tenderloin. On the grill is my favorite way to fix them. Here's how I do it.

Antelope Fillet

INGREDIENTS: One antelope tenderloin; one large garlic clove; coarse-ground pepper; 1 slice bacon per fillet.

Make your fillets about an inch and a half thick, sliced cross grain. Ring each fillet around its edge with a slice of bacon pinned down with a toothpick. Crush the garlic clove and rub the top of each fillet with it. Shake some pepper on next. Put the seasoned side of the fillet down on the grill and then season the other side.

Like most game, antelope is at its best if served a little bit rare, so when you see reddish juices oozing to the surface of the meat, turn the fillets. Wait for the juice to come up on the browned side. When it does, the fillets are done. A little shake of salt and they're ready to eat. Here at home we like fillets served with corn on the cob, tossed salad, and sourdough garlic bread.

Chatham's Roast Duck

If I were ever unlucky enough to find myself awaiting execution, about to eat my last meal, I would request that it be roast wild duck. Not just any old roast duck but wild duck roasted according to the recipe of fly fisherman and watercolor artist Russell Chatham. I will relate it directly, as best I can recall.

Waterfowling has been my passion for many years now. It is a pastime with a rich and broad tradition. The many facets of it — the dogs, guns, decoys, calls, blinds, boats and, most of all, the birds — are endlessly fascinating to those of us who head for the marshes and rivers each fall.

Some folks consider waterfowlers lunatics, for what sane person would rise at 3:00 a.m., don bulky, foul-smelling clothes and sit in a drafty duck blind with a polar wind blowing through it? I can only answer that those who ask have never watched and heard a marsh come to life at dawn, thrilled to the sight of mallards rocking into their decoys on cupped wings, or swelled with pride as a great-hearted retriever put a bird in their hand.

When I was living in Montana as a single man, I was known as "the duck bum." Several of my friends and I formed a loose association we jokingly referred to as the Valley Garden Duck Club. The name derived from the area we most frequently hunted. We built a blind on an island in the Madison River from materials we scrounged from a ranch dump. Some of the finest hours I can remember were passed in that blind.

Looking back, I recall the incident of the decoy stalker. It was midway through the duck and goose season. The hunting pace had slowed. Local ducks were wise to us and the northern birds had yet to arrive. There were four of us in the blind that morning, and nothing was flying. We sat and drank coffee, watched the sky, and speculated on where to set up our elk camp.

After quite some time, somebody spotted a little wad of about a half dozen mallards. I blew a short hail call and the ducks swung our way to give us a look. I switched to hen quacks and a feeding chuckle as the birds circled the blind. It looked like we were in for

Chatham's Roast Duck

some action when they cupped their wings and came straight in.

Just as they were at the edge of shotgun range, though, they flared wildly and pulled for the blue sky. In a jiffy they were gone. It didn't make sense. Our setup was right. The decoys looked good. As it turned out, they looked too good.

The ducks had shied away from a man wading in the river. We saw him moments later as he appeared beside our island, intently stalking our decoy spread with shotgun at the ready. As he was poised to cut down on them, I said, "Good morning." From the way he jumped, I'd be willing to bet a box of shells that he had to scoop out the seat of his waders later. His face turned fire engine red as reality dawned on him. Duped by our decoys, he hadn't spotted us in our ratty little blind.

As we deliberated on whether or not to shoot him, I took note of his outfit. He looked like he just stepped out of a sporting goods store and into the river. Everything he had on was spanking new. To top off his ensemble, he had a scoped deer rifle slung across his back. Deer season was on too, so I assumed he was looking for the first legal target of opportunity. I assumed right.

"Seen any deer?" he inquired.

I'll say this for him, he had more guts than a man could hang on a fence. We told he we hadn't seen any deer. Then he asked if there was a shallow spot where he could ford the river. We told him there was and gave him directions. He waded off toward the far bank. If he'd have stuck to our directions, he'd have made it alright, but half way out he lost his nerve and turned for a smaller island that sat below ours. Any river man knows the upstream end of an island will have a deep hole scooped out by the current. We yelled a warning, but to no avail. Six feet from dry ground, he disappeared.

Two seconds later his head popped up, followed by the rest of him, jettisoning equipment right and left. Pitching first his shotgun and then his rifle up on the bank, he hauled his soaking hulk out after them.

Chatham's Roast Duck

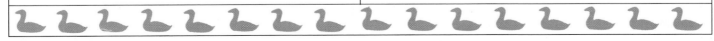

Gathering his weapons, he faded into the willows.

I wish I could tell you that we rushed down there and built a fire and got him out of his wet duds, that we gave him hot coffee from our thermos and loaned him a pair of dry socks. But we didn't. The poor dumb sod had flared the only ducks we'd seen all day, and sympathy did not abide in us.

We did eventually bring home a few ducks, though, and thanks to the generosity of Russ Chatham in sharing his recipe, here's how we dealt with them.

INGREDIENTS: One large duck per person (mallard, pintail, etc.); red wine (a mountain burgundy works best); fresh garlic cloves; one fresh lemon; cayenne pepper; Worcestershire sauce; butter; Currant jelly; olive oil.

Pick your birds as thoroughly as possible. Then singe the un-pickable pin feathers on a hot stove element. This also serves to snug up the skin to the carcass. Next, rub the outside of the bird all over with olive oil and then shake a little garlic powder on the breast.

Now, I know you're wondering about stuffing. There ain't any! You want the heat of the oven to get into the body cavity and cook from the inside. The bird must cook fast, sealing in juices and browning the skin. A duck cooked too long will dry out and be tough. You want that duck pink along the keel bone. So turn your oven up to 500 degrees and roast the bird for 25 minutes, breast side up. If you put several ducks in the same pan, don't let them touch each other. I like individual loaf pans.

While the birds are roasting, prepare the dipping sauce. Pour three cups of red wine in a sauce pan on low heat. Add a good-sized pat of butter and a crushed garlic clove and let it simmer. Next, put in one tablespoon of currant jelly, one tablespoon of Worcestershire sauce, and two teaspoons of freshly squeezed lemon juice. Add just a light dusting of cayenne. At the table, dip each bite of duck in this sauce, which you'll serve in individual cups at each plate. My favorite side dishes are a mix of long grain and wild rice, broccoli or asparagus, and garlic bread. This is a feast of grand dimensions.

Nick's Frybread

The plain truth is this: At any given time, I'd rather be horse packing in the mountains than anything else I can think of. This recipe comes from the first pack trip I ever went on, above Lake Tahoe in the Sierras. Nick Pazis and I borrowed a couple of horses from a fellow I worked with, and rode up toward Round Lake as soon as the snow melted enough to let us into the high country. I believe it was June of '69. It was before backpacking became a national craze, and you could still ride for half a day and pretty well isolate yourself.

Without a pack animal, we had to travel light. Some dry grub in our saddlebags and a couple of bed rolls was about the extent of our outfit. You could always count on the cutthroats to bite, so we figured to eat good. I even had a little three-cup coffee pot to make camp life complete.

The morning was perfect when we saddled our mounts and left Smith's place. The horses' feet slung diamond droplets into the early sun as we rode across the upper Truckee River and climbed out of Christmas Valley. Both Nick and I decided to take advantage of this trip to quit smoking, so neither of us had packed any cigarettes. I wasn't all that addicted, but Nick had the craving on him before we'd gotten two miles up the trail.

We switched back and forth through the timber as we gained altitude. It was big tree country with Ponderosa and Jeffrey pines, and not much understory. You can see a long way through those open woods, and I spotted movement about one hundred fifty yards up ahead. We reined in our horses to see what was up.

Down the trail came a man and a woman on foot. They carried fly rods and were dressed to the nines in fancy sporting duds. As they got closer, I could see they were older folks, sixtyish or so. Spotting us, they picked up their pace a little. When they were within twenty yards, the hailed us: "Have you seen a forest ranger?" He was flushed and excited and the lady looked scared. I told him we'd met no rangers on our way in.

The reason for all this commotion was a dead man. The old gentleman explained that he and his wife had been fishing their way up the creek that parallels the trail and had come upon a corpse in the water. "And I don't mind telling you, it's ruined our fishing trip!"

We agreed that would sure do it, alright. "Well, we're going to alert the authorities," he said. "I marked the trail opposite the creek where we found him. He's off to the right of the marker."

Nick's Frybread

As they made a move to leave, Nick spoke up. "Say, you don't happen to have a spare smoke on you?" The couple looked astonished. The man frowned darkly and only said "No!" They took off in a huff. "Jeez, Nick," I asked, "Where's your sense of propriety?" He looked at me matter-of-factly and answered, "Down at the truck with my pack of cigarettes."

As we took to the trail again, I wondered about the poor fellow up ahead. What had killed him? The creek was barely deep enough to hold a trout. It would take a determined effort to drown in it. Maybe he'd been shot by accident last deer season. If so, he'd be a little worse for wear by now. Or perhaps he'd taken the steep trail too fast and had a heart attack. My speculations were running wild when I saw the little arrow made of sticks pointing into the timber to the right.

We pulled up and, without the noise of horseshoes on rocks, I could clearly hear the sound of the creek. It was out of sight in the trees but less than a hundred yards away. Nick and I looked at each other. Except for a couple of old aunts and grannies at the funeral home, neither of us had ever seen a dead body. "What do you think?" Nick asked. I sat my horse as my curiosity fought with my sense of revulsion. "Might as well check him out," I answered.

With the horses tied just inside the timber, we took uncertain steps in the direction pointed out by the marker arrow. It felt like time was standing still; hours seemed to pass before I caught sight of the water. Scanning upstream and down, I saw nothing in the creek except an old rotten log. Something was wrong with the log, though, 'cause it was wearing blue jeans, boots and a leather vest. As we came to the edge of the bank, I could imagine the fishing oldsters walking up on this scene unaware. We, at least, had been warned.

He lay on his back, parallel to the current, only partly submerged. Mercifully for us, his right arm was crossed over his face, obscuring it from view. Judging from the exposed skin of his hand, we were right glad that his face was covered. But it wasn't really a grim or shocking sight. The body didn't resemble anything human, anything that had ever possessed life. It was just so much old stuff.

Later I learned that this unlucky fellow had been a fugitive from justice who had attempted to make a run for it through the mountains the previous winter. Trouble was, he had been to a party last thing before making his break and had tanked up on booze and pills. It was theorized that when he arrived at the

Nick's Frybread

creek it was partly canopied over with snow. In attempting a crossing, he'd broken through and been too loaded to get up.

It didn't take long for Nick and I to get our fill of the picture before us. I was poised to head back to the horses when I had a thought. "Say, Nick, you probably ought to check him for smokes, don't you think?"

"Well, I imagine if he's got any on him," Nick replied with a deadpan expression, "they're most likely too soggy to light."

We nervously chuckled a little, but our friend in the creek didn't seem embarrassed. You got to admit, a situation like this calls for a bit of comic relief.

We left the poor scoundrel to his long sleep and rode on up to Round Lake. There was a little height of boulders with a flat top above the shoreline, and we made our camp on it. There was still plenty of daylight, so after staking the horses in the lush mountain grass, I took rod in hand to fetch some small eating trout. By the time I got back to the fire with my catch, Nick had a good bait of frybread making. This is how he does it.

INGREDIENTS: Pre-mixed in a large plastic freezer bag, 3 cups all-purpose flour, 1 tablespoon baking powder, 2 tablespoons nonfat dry milk; packed separately, 2 tablespoons liquid shortening; 1/2 tablespoon oil or margarine (pan greasing).

Blend the liquid shortening with the dry ingredients, then mix in about one and a half cups water, with dry milk added, to make a stiff dough. Form into a round, flat loaf and put in a greased skillet. Place in a medium hot area of the fire and peek under it periodically with your spatula. When it is a nice golden brown, flip it over. Repeat the inspection procedure. When it's nicely browned on both sides, it should be done in the middle. Slice into pie wedges and butter it up. Serves two to four, depending on how hungry everybody is.

Cameron Lake Steak

You may not think a recipe for something as simple as grilled beefsteak is necessary in a modern cookbook. I might agree if I hadn't been served so many poorly handled examples of that All-American classic. So, I'll share another little slice of Montana cuisine with you.

In the spring of '79 I was newly married and working on a ranch south of Ennis. It was a cow-and-calf operation that ran about three hundred head of mother cows. The ranchers grew their own hay, too. In the foothills of the Rockies, it was a spectacular setting and a beautiful place to work.

The pay for married men was $600 a month, a beef a year, and a house to live in. It didn't sound like a lot, and it wasn't. But the house was cozy and we got to keep our personal saddle horses in a pasture beside the house. Our son liked it fine. He had the run of the place. The following recipe, in fact, is dedicated to him.

Justin was my bonus for getting married. He was seven when I started courting Shirley, and he was a pistol. With more energy than a sackful of monkeys, he made life interesting at all times. Shortly after we were married, Shirley began to lobby for me to fill Justin in on the facts of life.

I'd never given a birds and bees lecture before, so, like most parents, I was a little reluctant to get started. And like most parents I put it off. But Justin, like most kids, started bringing home reports of what he'd heard from his compadres at school. Some of it was funny, and some of it was truly amazing. I decided it was time to set the record straight.

Back in the hills behind the house, about two miles in and higher up, was Cameron Lake. It's a pretty little alpine jewel, and I figured to take Justin up there for an overnighter and give him the true skinny on matters reproductive. As far as he was concerned it was just another sleep-out.

On a bright, balmy Saturday, after my morning chores were done, we saddled my big mare and his little gelding and rode out the yard gate for the lake. It was a short ride, and we were in no hurry. Justin got Diamond as a Christmas present the previous winter, and the two of them were getting along

Cameron Lake Steak

famously. Diamond wasn't much to look at, but he was double tough and smooth to ride. A pretty good kinda kid's horse.

We made the lake early in the afternoon. After locating a campsite and dumping our gear, we took a little scouting ride around. I was stalling and I knew it. All the way in I'd been mentally working on what I was going to say, searching for some sort of analogy that an eight-year-old boy would understand.

Suddenly, it came to me. Our dog, Mr. March, was named in honor of a fine old bird dog trainer who was a friend and mentor in my youth. Mr. March was a golden retriever, a fine duck and goose dog. Friends of ours in town had a part black Lab named Pearl. Earlier in the spring, Pearl had come into season. Our friends didn't want to spay her, and they knew that sooner or later Pearl would get loose and go a-courtin'. They decided the best thing was to bring her out to the ranch and let Mr. March do the

honors. That way they'd get a well-bred litter they wouldn't get stuck with. So Pearl came to visit for a week, and Justin just happened to witness the nuptials.

Anyway, I figured I would use the honeymoon rites of Pearl and Mr. March as an analogy of the human process, so we rode back to our camp and I got a fire going. As the wood burned down to cooking coals, I launched into my lesson.

"Say, Justin," I asked, "Have you ever wondered how people make babies?"

"No," he answered.

"Well, would you like to know?"

"I guess so." He didn't sound too enthusiastic, but now I was committed.

"Well, you remember when Pearl came out to visit Mr. March a while back?" He said he did. "Do you remember how they made Pearl's puppies?" He said he did. "Well, that's pretty much how people do it, too."

Cameron Lake Steak

He got a real thoughtful look on his face and stared intently across the lake. I began to think that maybe he had spotted something on the far shore. Then, he inquired, "Do people get stuck together, too?"

To this day I am proud of myself for not laughing out loud, because inside I was convulsing. "Yes, Son," I said, "sometimes they get stuck for thirty or forty years."

When the coals were ready, I got my little camp grill and the T-bones out of the saddle bags. Now here's how you do Cameron Lake Steak.

INGREDIENTS: One T-bone, New York, or Ribeye steak per person; garlic clove, sliced into slivers; coarse ground black pepper; salt to taste.

Burn a fire of dry pine limbs down to cooking coals. Burn plenty so you won't run out of heat before steaks are done. Make a few punctures in each steak with a knife, and stick garlic slivers in each hole. Sprinkle black pepper on one side of each steak and place them seasoned side down on the grill. If you like steak medium rare, look for the red juice coming to the surface. When it does, turn the meat and pepper the top side. When the juice surfaces again, it's done. Salt to taste. The wood smoke gives the steak a special flavor.

Trout Omelette

A few years back, I lived about five minutes by pickup truck from one of the hottest trout pools in the state of Montana. It's known locally as the "Million Dollar Hole." Whenever I had a craving for a few small trout for the table, that's where I'd head. Not that there weren't big fish too, but I only kept those under ten inches. If I felt like a special breakfast, I'd collect a couple of these little eaters and whip up a trout omelette. But before I tell you how to assemble this dish, let me talk about that fishing hole.

Have you ever been in a blizzard of bugs? Most any July afternoon on this particular piece of water you could count on a caddis hatch that would almost choke you. Size 14s and 16s so thick in the air that half of them seemed to go up your nose. So many bugs on the water that keeping track of your fly was a real challenge. The rises coming so frequently that you'd swear a hundred kids were up on the bank, shooting into the water with BB guns.

More than a hole, this was really a long, cigar-shaped pool paralleled by an equally long riffle. The whole affair was more than 300 yards from end to end, and you could stand in the riffle, at the edge of the deep water, and cast to rising fish in the pool, all the way to the far bank. If you fished it right, you could spend most of the day on that one stretch.

At the peak of summer, it stays light 'til after 10:30 p.m. in that country. I remember more than one night there, fishing in the dark and setting my hook by the little sucking sound made by the striking trout. If you can imagine wading back to your truck after midnight, you can appreciate the kind of fishing it was.

I remember a day spent down on that stretch with Chuck Kneib, a river guide and fishing friend. Chuck is a first class fly caster, and he was hooking three fish to my one. That's not to say I wasn't doing well. It's just that Chuck is deadly. The trout were about two-thirds rainbows and the rest browns. Most were from 12 to 16 inches long, but we were releasing everything. The caddis hatch was coming off in grand style.

The day slipped by in fishing glory, and before we knew it, the sun was behind the mountain, and the air began to cool. I waded over toward Chuck to see if he'd had enough. He agreed it was about time to hang it up, and we were making motions to leave

Trout Omelette

when I spotted a drift boat coming down the current. One man was rowing the boat, another stood up front in the knee locks, casting.

As the distance narrowed, we recognized the man handling the rod. It was another local guide, whom I'll not name. He was an older fellow and one of the senior fishing guides on the river. Six-foot-four and as big as a barn, he had an ego to match. Famed for his good opinion of himself, he was fishing from his own boat while his paying client rowed. I was astonished. Chuck just shook his head.

After getting off the river, we stopped at one of the local water holes for a beer and a burger. Half way through our second mug, the big guide waltzed in like the Duke of Paducah. As he passed us on his way to the dining room, Chuck stopped him.

"How do you manage to get your dude to row for you?"

The old guide smiled and answered, "Some folks just like to watch me fish."

Back to the recipe. This is how to do a Trout Omelette.

INGREDIENTS: One small trout, 8 to 10 inches in length; three large eggs; $1/2$ of a small white onion; 4 small, fresh mushrooms; one tablespoon ripe olive slices; one large pat butter; three tablespoons whole milk; cooking oil; coarse ground black pepper; salt.

Pan fry the trout in the oil. When done, peel the skin and flake meat from the bone. Set the meat aside. Now chop the onion and slice the mushrooms. In a clean skillet, saute the onions, mushrooms, and olives in butter. While these are cooking, beat the eggs, with the milk, in a bowl.

When the sauteed stuff is done enough to suit you, scatter it evenly in the skillet and carefully pour the beaten eggs in. They should cover the bottom of the pan without disturbing the sauteed stuff. When the egg begins to thicken, distribute the flaked trout on the egg on one side of the skillet. As soon as the egg is firm enough, fold the half without the trout over that half that has it. Cook for about another minute. Serves one real hungry person or two normal folks.

Cascade Cutthroats

My first trip to Yellowstone Park was in the early fall of 1969. It was after Labor Day, most of the rubber-neckers had gone home, and the weather was perfect. I spent three days driving around, doing some rubber-necking of my own. The elk were bugling, the swans were flying, and I was sure I had died and that this was heaven.

I wanted to backpack into one of the many lakes off the blacktop and do some fishing. When I got a map at one of the gift shops, I found out that a campfire permit was required. They were available at any of the ranger stations, so I went looking for one.

The young lady in Smoky Bear green asked me which lake I had picked to visit. As she issued my fire permit, she pointed out that Cascade Lake, my choice, was in a grizzly bear area. She then heaped a pile of warning literature on me. It included instructions for moving camp far from cooking areas, hanging food in trees separate from sleeping areas, how to roll into a ball and play dead while a bear chews on and then buries you, and so on. By the time I got to the bottom of the stack of pamphlets, the hair on the back of my neck was standing straight up.

But I was determined to hike to Cascade Lake. It was only two miles up the trail, and that suited my time frame. Parking my old Chevy wagon and loading my pack for an overnighter, I started in.

The first mile and a half was through open lodgepole pine stands, and I half expected a grizzly to rise up out of the ground and knock me flat. In reality, nothing larger than a ground squirrel crossed my path. The terrain was mostly level, and the country went by fairly quickly. Timber gave way to open parkland, and I could see the lake a half mile up ahead. It was small, only five acres or so, and lay in a shallow basin.

There were trout rising when I dropped my pack beside the trail. I put my rod together and, as the old-timers say, I "went amongst 'em." In a few casts I had three fat cutthroats for my supper. While cleaning them at lakeside, I looked across the meadow to see a large, dark shape that hadn't been there before. I immediately thought "bear," but it was a long ways out and I couldn't be sure. After watching it a while I decided it was a cow moose. But I wasn't positive.

I cooked and ate supper right there. Then I moved to the other end of the lake to escape the smell of fried

Cascade Cutthroats

fish. A deeply worn trail circled the lake. It was full of bear tracks. Black bear or grizzly I couldn't tell, but bear nonetheless. A little nervous, I gathered up a big slug of firewood and got a blaze going.

After making coffee, I pulled the pot off the fire and heaped more wood on the coals. My wood pile was getting low and I didn't want to turn in yet, so I took my flashlight and headed for the blowdown I had been breaking limbs off of for fuel.

The night was black as pitch, and my stomach was a little tight as I left the security of the fire. No guns are allowed in the park — the most potent weapon I had was the flashlight. The blowdown was just coming into view when I heard something crashing in the brush to my right. It sounded like an out-of-control bus.

My mind's eye played a movie as I turned the light toward the source of the racket. The movie had a cast of two, myself and a ten-foot grizzly. The action consisted of me standing slack jawed while the bear knocked my head off with one swipe of his massive paw. As my mental epic continued with the bear dining on my corpse, the flashlight beam located the source of the noise. Waddling off with an air of disdain was a porcupine the size of a Shetland pony.

When my pulse dropped below two hundred, I picked up an armload of wood and returned to the fire. After a change of shorts, I went to bed. If any bears did visit me that night, they let me be. I caught another skilletful of trout the next morning and had them for breakfast before pulling out, and here's the recipe for Cascade Cutthroats.

INGREDIENTS: Two 8- to 12-inch cutthroat trout (or browns, brookies or rainbows) per person; one egg per three fish; cornmeal; cayenne pepper; ground dill weed; cooking oil.

Beat eggs thoroughly in a shallow bowl. Dip fish in the egg, covering the entire fish. Next, roll fish in the cornmeal, getting as much stuck to the fish as you can. Heat three-quarters of an inch of oil in your skillet. Lay fish in hot oil. Sprinkle a little cayenne (damn little, it's hot!) and ground dill on the topside of fish. Six or seven minutes per side should do it. After turning, sprinkle cayenne and dill on browned side. Serve hot out of the frying pan. Be sure and eat the skin. It's good.

Neck Beans

Venison is too good to waste. Now that we've established that, let's talk about a cut of meat that frequently gets wasted. The neck from a buck deer often gets thrown out with the head, especially if the buck was rutting when taken. It's a shame. There are a number of things you can do with the meat from a deer's neck, such as cut it up chunk-style for stew, dice it for chili, or grind it up for spaghetti sauce.

There's one additional use for neck meat that's my personal favorite. Whenever I bring home a buck, I like to fix neck beans. Pinto beans go well with venison, but you can use most any kind of beans you like. This recipe is the best I know of for masking the sometimes musky flavor of venison taken from a rutting buck. The first time I had occasion to try it was on a big trophy whitetail that I took in Montana about twelve years ago.

The duck and deer seasons run concurrently in that part of the country, and I made a habit of not going anywhere during that time without a shotgun and a rifle in the truck. You just never knew when you might run into some meat for the freezer. In those days I got as much of my table fare from the woods and waters as from the grocery, so I kept the tools of the trade close at hand.

The big buck was encountered on a duck hunt. I'd spent the day jump shooting on the upper Madison above Ennis Lake. My golden retriever and I had had a good day on the river and were wading back to the truck with several fat greenheads for the larder. Beau was my first retriever, trained partly by me, from books, but mostly by himself, from experience. He was small for the breed, only fifty pounds, but had enough heart for a dozen dogs. His job was retrieving whatever I shot, and he did it unconditionally.

I had parked my pickup between the river bank and a cutover barley field. A screen of brush grew along the fence line around the field, providing plenty of cover for deer and other game. As Beau and I came up out of the water, I spotted the biggest buck whitetail I'd ever seen. He stood out in the barley stubble, a hundred and fifty yards from the nearest cover. He spotted me at the same time but made no move to leave the field. By the look of his rut-swollen neck, I could imagine the reason for his lack of fear. It was as big around as a washtub. Buck deer can be

Neck Beans

notoriously unwary of danger during the mating season, and this old man was no exception.

It only took a second for me to size up the situation, and I quickly dropped out of sight and began a low crawl to the truck. Beau sensed that the hunt was suddenly on again, and he snuck along beside me. My .270 was on the front seat, and I traded my pumpgun for it as quietly as I could. Chambering a round, I made the crawl back to the fence line. Along the way I thought that most likely the buck had quit the field by now. But not so. There he stood, not having moved a step. I couldn't believe my luck.

As I poked my rifle through the weeds growing along the fence row, the deer seemed to be staring right at me. I knew he wouldn't stick around forever. The range was about 125 yards, and the buck dropped to the shot. I was patting myself on the back when out of the corner of my eye I saw a golden streak pass by me. Beau had been at my side for this entire episode, and he was used to having a job to do whenever he heard the report of a gun. When my

rifle cracked and the buck fell, Beau just naturally dashed out to fetch.

I tried to call him off, but without effect. He covered the distance in a jiffy, and without hesitation took a grip on the deer by one haunch, trying to lift him. Of course he couldn't, so he hunched up and tried to drag him backwards, also with no results. At that point he went to bucking and jumping in frustration, never releasing his hold.

As all this was going on, I was hurrying to the scene. When I arrived, Beau was still locked to the buck. Laying down my rifle, I gently pried the brave little retriever loose from his quarry. I had to hold him for a minute to calm him down as he strained to get back into the game. Finally, he relaxed and I let him go. He stepped to the deer and took a sniff, then looked up at me as if to say, "Sorry, Boss, but this duck is just too big."

Up close, the deer was a real eye opener. His rack was thick and high and had four points to a side. Heavy bodied and in perfect condition, he would

Neck Beans

grace my table for many a good meal. The sun was down and the air had a sharp bite to it when I finished the field dressing.

I hung him in a shed for about ten days to age the meat. He stayed cool without freezing in the moderate temperatures of early fall. It's a good idea, I think, to hang a mature buck for a good while to tenderize him, especially if he was rutting when taken, as this one was. When I skinned him out at the end of the aging period, his neck looked like an oil drum. I butchered the carcass, double wrapped the neck in freezer paper, wrote "neck beans" on the outside of the package, and put it in the deep freeze.

The steaks went first, then the chops and roasts. When I'd worked my way through the burger and stew meat, there was that lonely old neck staring up at me from the bottom of the freezer. A trip to the store for a bag of pinto beans and I was ready to do up a big pot of neck beans like this:

INGREDIENTS: One deer neck, removed from carcass between shoulders and skull; two large garlic cloves, quartered; $1/2$ teaspoon powdered cumin;

1 large bay leaf; a healthy dash of cayenne pepper; two large white onions, cut into eighths; $1/2$ teaspoon salt; one large bag pinto beans.

Soak your beans overnight in a large stew pot. If the neck is from a large deer, a five-gallon pot is not too big. In the morning, pour off the soaking water and rinse the beans thoroughly. If you have two big pots, it doesn't hurt to soak the neck overnight in salt water as well. Next, trim all fat and surface membrane from the meat. Put the neck and beans in your largest pot with a gallon of fresh water and bring to a boil.

Now turn the heat to simmer and add the remaining ingredients. Leave the bay leaf whole so you can remove it when serving. Continue to simmer for four to six hours. The meat will be falling apart, so strip it off with a fork and discard the bone. Stir the pot well before serving. A little Louisiana Red Hot really tops off this dish, if you like hot stuff. I usually fire up a batch of cornbread to go with neck beans.

Grouse on the Grill

This entree dates from my first trip to the northern Rockies. I was living at Georgetown Lake, about 20 miles out of Anaconda, Montana. I'd rented a motel room for a month, off-season rates being low enough to suit my budget. It was mid-October and most of the rooms went empty each night. I had a kitchenette with a big double sink for cleaning fish and game, so I was as happy as a clam.

I was building a porch for the lady who owned the motel, but since the trout fishing season and duck season were both on, there was more to tend than just carpenter work. My daily schedule went something like this: My alarm would go off at 7:00 a.m. I'd fix a little bait of breakfast and be down by the pump house on the lake shore at eight. An underwater spring bubbled up about 50 feet off shore, and plenty of trout hung out in this little honey hole. I'd stick around long enough to haul in two or three fat rainbows, then go back to the motel and be on the job by nine. A few hours of porch building and I'd be ready for lunch, usually taken in the motel bar. Back to work 'til about 3:30 in the afternoon, and then down to the mill cove to welcome the evening flight of ducks. Next, a supper of pan-fried trout or roast duck in my room, followed by one last call at the bar for a beer or three. Finally, an hour with Louis

Lamour by bed lamp, and then lights out. Some sack time under an open window in the sweet mountain air completed the cycle. It was a strenuous routine and no doubt would have killed a lesser man.

I'd been at the lake about a week when I met a fellow who worked for the state's wildlife agency. He was taking creel censuses, which entailed checking fishermen's catches for number, species, and length of fish. He wasn't a game warden and didn't check licenses, but told me that some people ran from him anyway. He suspected they were violators who mistook him for the law.

He was a personable sort, and we soon struck up a friendship. He'd been stationed at a one room log house owned by Montana Game and Fish. A little creek ran past it on its way to the lake, and he invited me up to try the fishing. The creek was alive with pan-sized brook trout, and they wanted to play. It took about an hour to catch enough for a two-man feed, and when I got back to the cabin, my new friend had the skillet hot.

(I wish I could remember the guy's name, but I can't. He had a part Lab named Sako, but his name just doesn't come back to me. I always seem to remember the dogs.)

Grouse on the Grill

While we ate, Greg (I'll call him that) told me about his plan to take a scouting trip for elk the next day. The season was a week away, and it was time to decide where to hunt. Greg asked if I'd like to come along. Wanting to see some new country, I agreed. He recommended I bring a .22, as grouse season was open and we'd likely see a few. I had a .22 pistol and said I'd bring it along.

We met early next morning, had coffee, and then headed for the hills. Greg drove us into the Pintlar Range, a part of the Montana Rockies that hosted healthy populations of deer and elk. After a drive of an hour or so, we'd gone as far as two-wheel drive could take us. Gregg pulled off the logging road and parked, and we continued on foot. It was chilly in the timber, but the climbing warmed us and it felt good to be in the high country.

While Greg and I looked for elk sign, Sako was doing a thorough job of harassing every ground squirrel and chipmunk in the neighborhood. He was having the time of his life, and I envied him his four legs.

We poked around looking for tracks, rubs, wallows or anything else that would reveal the presence of elk. Whenever a game trail would cross the road, we inspected it for fresh tracks. Conditions were dry, though, making it rough for us to age what sign we did find. It began to look as if we would be wise to find another area for our hunting, come the season. After two miles of careful scouting, we were yet to cut a fresh track.

If that bothered us, Sako couldn't have cared less. He kept up his relentless pursuit of the chipmunks, certain in his heart that any second he was going to catch one of the pesky critters. The chipmunks seemed to enjoy the game as much as the dog.

We entered an area of deadfall timber and bear grass, and Greg mentioned that he'd hiked through the spot earlier in the season. He said that at that time he had seen several grouse. The words were barely out of his mouth when Sako, hot on the trail of a chipmunk, flushed two big spruce grouse. They flew into the branches of — what else? — a spruce. Sako paced about the base of the tree and looked up at the birds while they looked down at him.

Greg took aim with his scoped .22 rifle and dropped the bird on the right. Sako delivered it in proud Labrador fashion. The grouse on the left watched the goings-on with interest. I drew my revolver and, taking

Grouse on the Grill

precise aim, missed him cleanly. My second shot was true, though, and we had the makings of a good dinner.

Spruce grouse aren't famous for an abundance of gray matter, as was amply demonstrated in the next few minutes. Greg and I were turning to head back to the truck when something caught my eye. Peeking from behind the trunk of another tree was a third grouse, eyeing us with intense curiosity. I got Greg's attention and pointed the bird out to him. After his initial surprise, he raised his rifle and squeezed off a shot.

Feathers flew off the bird's neck, and it jerked its head back behind the tree trunk. So much for that grouse, I thought. But there came that head, popping back out for another look. Greg drew a bead and fired again. And again feathers cut from the bird's neck, and again the head jerked back. Surely we'd seen the last of that grouse, I told myself, but just moments later the head was again peering at us from around the tree. This bird was determined to see the bottom of a frying pan, and Greg's next shot was the charm. Sako fetched the grouse, and we all headed down the mountain.

Back at the cabin, it was time for Grouse on the Grill. This is how you do it:

INGREDIENTS: *One grouse per person (blue grouse, ruffed grouse, or spruce grouse); $1/4$-lb. stick of butter or margarine; 2 teaspoons Worchestershire sauce; juice of $1/2$ lemon; one large garlic clove; $1/2$ teaspoon finely ground black pepper.*

Split birds in half along the keel bone. When the coals are ready, place the unseasoned birds on the grill. (I like medium hot coals, like you might grill chicken over.) Turn the halves frequently so they don't burn.

Meanwhile, put the rest of the ingredients in a sauce pan. Crush the garlic clove first. Put the pan on one side of the grill, melting the butter and blending everything. Stir this, the basting sauce, every now and then.

When the birds are browning nicely, begin basting, first one side and then the other. When you think they're done, they probably are. Not having as much fat, grouse don't take as much cooking as chicken. A bit of salt to taste and the birds can be served.

Frank's Green Tomato Fry

Here's a concoction from my days at Georgetown Lake, Montana. The first time I saw the lake was on a trip through that country with Frank Sloan (see Sloan's Smoked Salmon). We were camping out of the back of my truck and had stopped to sample the trout fishing. There's a real nice state campground at the lake and we had a comfortable little setup.

We spent a couple of fine days on Georgetown, catching fish, eating fish, and generally being lazy. It was late September and the weather was as good as you could ask for, and Frank and I were in hog heaven. This was in the dark days before I discovered fly fishing, and I have to confess that we were quite happy to drown a number of night crawlers for the benefit of the 12- to 18-inch rainbows that seemed grateful to get them.

On the drive up from the Bitterroot Valley, we had stopped at a roadside produce stand. It offered a tempting selection from the rancher's garden: sweet corn, golden summer squash, tender young onions, and little green tomatoes. The price didn't amount to much, so we filled a couple of grocery bags.

I figure I gained at least five pounds in the two days we spent at the lake. When we weren't fishing, we were cooking. With the produce from the roadside stand, Frank put together a batch of good eating that I still haven't forgotten. He called it a green tomato fry, and it goes like this:

INGREDIENTS: Six small to medium size green tomatoes, cut into eighths; three medium-size white onions, also in eighths; four small summer squashes, sliced in rounds; four small to medium size ears white sweet corn; cooking oil; salt and pepper to taste.

Heat the oil in a large skillet (I prefer cast iron). About 1/4 inch in the bottom is plenty. I like olive oil, but if you don't, peanut oil is good, and corn oil is okay. Get the oil good and hot. Put the tomatoes in first; being green and hard, they take the longest to cook. Ten minutes later, add the squash. Slice the raw corn off the cob, catching the milky liquid, and add it, along with the onions, about five minutes after adding the squash.

After another five minutes at high heat, turn down heat to simmer. From this point, it's up to you when to call it done. I like my veggies firm, but you can cook it down almost to a mush and they'll still be good. Salt and pepper to taste. Serves four.

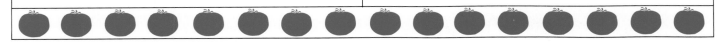

Desert Creek Gopher Kabobs

(Don't try this unless you have to!)

No doubt you've read about idiots who go into the wilderness with a minimum of provisions, determined to live off the country by taking game or catching fish. I'm here to tell you that those stories are true, because I was one of those idiots. This recipe, if I can honestly call it that, was born of starvation on a trip I took into the Nevada desert, on which I was reduced to eating gophers. It's a better story than it was a trip.

I was living near the California-Nevada border, a single man with a saddle horse and a craving for wild country. I had a few days off between carpentry jobs, and I figured I could use a dose of the back country. After hearing my plan, a horseman buddy of mine recommended a ride up Desert Creek. I had never heard of the place but soon learned about it from my friend. A lone mountain stood in the Nevada desert, in a fairly remote part of the state, and Desert Creek was the main drainage of this single peak. My friend claimed that the creek was full of pan-sized cutthroats. He loaned me his map, and I started getting ready.

Having only one horse, I had to pack my whole outfit on him. A saddle horse shouldn't have to be a pack horse too, so I was restricted to what would go in my saddle bags. A one-pound coffee can to boil water in, some coffee, a drinking cup, a pound and a half of home-made venison jerky, and a dozen wholewheat rolls. That and a sleeping bag tied behind the saddle was all of it. Putting my faith in the universal willingness of cutthroat trout to hop in a skillet, I loaded the gelding into my ratty old trailer and struck off.

The drive was pleasant enough. It was mostly new country to me, and there's always a hint of the unknown when travelling in fresh territory.

Just as advertised, there stood the lone peak looming in solitude. Covered with green timber and sagebrush, it appeared as though it just popped up from the desert floor. The creek issued from Lobdelle Lake, 26 miles upcountry from the trailhead. More than a trail, it was actually a pretty good dirt road, but I hadn't looked at the map close enough to notice. No matter, I was saddled up and ready to go, and it was a beautiful afternoon for a ride.

Desert Creek Gopher Kabobs

In my standard, organized fashion, I was getting a late start. Looking back, it seems there was some trouble catching the gelding from my leased pasture. Whatever the excuse, we'd only covered about six miles when we ran out of daylight. At the same time the sun was dropping behind the ridge, we rounded a bend in the road and were greeted by the sight of a campground, complete with Winnebago and family. So much for the allusion of pristine wilderness. At least they were the only outfit there, so I made my little camp on the other end of the clearing. There was good grass for the horse, and after stripping the gear off of him I staked him out to graze.

It was spring, and the air cooled quickly in the absence of the sun. I went to the creek to get water and was mighty depressed by what I found. Until now, the road had paralleled the creek from high above, and I hadn't gotten a close look at it. There I stood beside a mountain stream in full runoff, brimful to its banks with water the color of creamed coffee. Catching a fish from that gruel would be next to impossible. A little later by my fire, as I sat and chewed a piece of jerky, my stomach tightened with anticipation. This trip was going to get hungry.

As I sat and wondered about the future source of sustenance, an older fellow wandered up from the Winnebago. While shooting the breeze with him, I found out he was the patriarch of the bunch, and he wondered why I was up there on horseback when I could have driven. I responded with something spiritual about how I preferred horses to trucks, and he looked at me like the fool I felt. And, like a fool, I mentioned that the point of the trip was fishing. He replied that I better have plenty of other grub. I told him I had lots of it. Before leaving he invited me down for coffee and some fireside socializing. I thanked him and told him I'd be down directly.

Another piece of jerky and a wheat roll completed my supper ration. It did not appease my hunger, however. I looked out at my gelding filling himself with rich mountain grass. God! how I envied that horse right then. I walked him down to the creek for a drink, restaked him, and wandered over to the

Desert Creek Gopher Kabobs

Winnebago. After drinking a cup of coffee, and satisfying everyone's curiosity as to why I was up there on horseback when I could have driven, I returned to my own little camp and hit the sack.

I slept soundly and woke with first light. Sitting up in my bag, a quick look around told me something was missing. It turned out to be my horse. I'd tied him to a sagebrush about fifty feet from where I slept, and there was now a hole in the ground where the bush used to be. Sage roots don't go very deep, as was so graphically illustrated. I was a little smarter for this experience . . . and on foot. I figured the gelding wouldn't go back farther than he had walked in. Of course, I had to walk six miles back down the mountain on no breakfast, and the exercise did wonders for my appetite. I rode back to camp at a lope.

After more jerky and a couple of rolls, the horse and I continued on toward the lake. I kept my eyes on the creek, hoping to see it clear up as we climbed higher, but it just wasn't happening. The realization that no fish would likely be forthcoming seemed to fuel my hunger even more. My jerky and rolls were all gone before lunch time, and I didn't feel like I'd eaten at all.

I had brought along a .22 rifle, and I started taking potshots at jay birds and anything else that looked edible. But my stomach was growling so bad that I couldn't hit a thing. I considered eating the horse, but walking out to the truck was less appealing than going hungry.

We travelled on toward the lake all afternoon, me praying for the appearance of a rabbit or a grouse, but none were to be seen. I held out hope that the lake would be clear and fishable, and on we rode. I was about ready to stop and roast one of my boots when I saw something lying in the trail ahead. It looked like a crumpled paper bag, and I guessed it was just some litter dropped by a careless hiker. When we got close enough, I could see it was a cookie bag, and I was sure it would be empty. But I got down to check.

Manna from heaven! The label said "Mother's Cookies," and it was half full. Where could it have come from? It must have fallen from the sky because we were now twenty miles in and hadn't seen a soul since the Winnebago campers. I was giddy with gratitude and bolted down half the contents before

Desert Creek Gopher Kabobs

getting a grip on myself. I said a silent thanks to "Mother" for dropping the cookies (miniature chocolate chip) into my path. After rolling up the paper sack and stuffing it into the saddle bags, I mounted and continued on toward the lake.

Well into the afternoon, we finally arrived at Lobdelle Lake. It was a man-made reservoir situated in a little bowl near the top of the mountain, and it was as muddy as the creek. I felt like riding the horse on in and drowning myself. Instead, I got out the fishing gear and gave it the old college try. While I sat on the bank waiting for a nibble, I vacuumed up the rest of the cookies, to the last, subatomic particle. I don't recall eating the bag, so I must not have.

Of course, I never got even a hint of a bite. The top of the mountain was bare of timber, and a stiff wind added a vigorous chop to the muddy water. The deck was stacked against me, so I reeled in and headed down the mountain.

A couple of miles down the back trail was a bald, grassy ridge. It was formed by a gently rounded shoulder of the mountain and offered a fine view of the desert below. Stopping the horse, I took a moment to soak up the scene and listen to my stomach growl. There were little golf-ball-sized holes scattered all around, and soon as we had been still for a bit, gophers began to pop up everywhere. Tying the horse to the first available tree, I snatched the .22 out of the scabbard and started blazing away. My aim was little better than before, but when the rifle was empty and the smoke had cleared, everybody was back underground except three unfortunates, which I quickly gathered for an on-the-spot supper.

After building a sagebrush fire, I dressed my game. Now I don't recommend making a habit of eating gophers, but if you're hungry enough, they fill the void. This is more of a method than a recipe, but here goes anyway:

Desert Creek Gopher Kabobs

INGREDIENTS: Two or more gophers per starving soul; a green stick, sharpened; a bed of hot coals; some salt, if you've got it.

Dress and skin the gophers as you would a rabbit or squirrel. Save any little bits of fat that may be on the carcass, because if you're hungry enough to eat these guys in the first place, you want every available calorie you can get. If it's a true survival situation with no relief in sight, eat the entrails, too.

Once they're cleaned, impale the gophers on your stick and prop them over the hot coals. If you really are starving, try to catch the juice that drips off and get it down, too. Every little bit helps. Turn frequently so they won't burn. When the meat is well browned all over, they're done. Being small critters, they don't take too long to cook. Salt lightly and eat right off the bone. You'll be shocked how good they taste. Remember, hunger is the best sauce.

P.S. As soon as I got off that mountain I stopped at the first roadside market I came to and spent a small fortune on junk food. By the time I got home I was sick as a dog.

Chicken Fried Rattlesnake

Lots of folks cringe at the thought of seeing a snake, much less eating one. But the fact is that snake meat, particularly rattlesnake, is finely textured, flaky, and delicious. Snakes are also easy to clean, if it's done before they cool and stiffen.

I remember a certain rattlesnake that wound up in my skillet a few years ago. Shirley and I were up at our cabin site working on our log-house-in-progress. It sat on an open bench below the foothills of the Gravelly Range, in southwest Montana, an area known to grow a few rattlers.

We were framing the roof, notching and putting up pole rafters, when Shirley excused herself for a nature call. There was no plumbing or outhouse yet, but with the nearest neighbor a half mile away, she just walked down to the rim of the creek canyon to water the buffalo grass. I kept working.

Five minutes later I heard her very quietly calling me. She was a hundred yards away, and I could barely understand what she was saying. Something about a snake, and would I come down there and bring my gun. In that country I never went out from town without some sort of firearm. Going to my truck for my .357, I heard her call again. I hustled down the canyon rim to see what was up.

She calmly stood back from a little rock shelf, maybe twenty feet away. About to relieve herself, she'd heard the rattling in the rocks, only four feet from the chosen spot. She eased back, and the snake slid under the shelf. The rattling instantly took her back, she said, to a time when her dad, in order to warn his baby girl, had shaken a tobacco sack containing snake rattles by her ear. He told her that if she ever heard that sound, she should freeze. She did.

I peered carefully under the rocks until I spotted the snake. Ordinarily, I don't kill snakes out of hand, but this one was a little too close to the cabin. I shot it and pulled it out. The skin became a hatband and the meat an entree to a good supper. This is how to chicken fry a rattlesnake.

INGREDIENTS: One rattlesnake, dressed and skinned; seasoned flour; cooking oil; salt and pepper to taste.

Chicken Fried Rattlesnake

To clean the snake, cut off the tail and head. (First, of course, be absolutely sure the snake is, in fact, dead. Then, still be careful of the fangs when cutting off the head. You wouldn't want to get snakebit as a result of your own clumsiness.) Save the rattles. Now, slit the belly from end to end. With the tip of your knife, get under the skin on the head end and begin working it back. When you've got a couple of inches free, get a grip on it and pull straight back toward the tail. The skin will slip right off. The entrails remain in the rib cage, encased in a membrane sack. It pops right out in one piece. Save the skin for a hatband or belt.

Now, rinse the carcass and wash your hands. Cut the body into segments three inches long and roll them in the seasoned flour, covering them completely. Pour oil an inch deep into a skillet and get it good and hot, but not smoking. Lay chunks, meaty side down, in the oil. Turn once after five or six minutes. It's done when golden brown. Salt and pepper to taste. Serve with whatever you like to have with fried fish or chicken.

Duck Blind Dogs

One of the joys of duck hunting from a blind is the charcoal bucket. It not only warms cold feet and hands, it makes a handy grill for cooking hot lunch between flights. And one of the most frequent items to cross the duck hunter's grill is the always popular hot dog, wiener, frankfurter, tube steak, or whatever you call them. This recipe was borrowed from a waterfowler friend of mine named Bill White, the best caller I ever hunted with, and is dedicated to my first Labrador retriever, Tank. A big black dog with a lion's heart and a lamb's temperament, he has gone to the Big Marsh beyond. But while he was here, he was one hell of a duck dog.

The particular hunt from which this recipe came was not what you'd call a barnburner. There were a few ducks around, but nothing much was flying. We'd managed to scratch down a couple of greenheads, but the action was very slow. Mostly we sat and told jokes. Tank sat in his corner of the blind, looking bored.

Bill fired up the charcoal bucket and put the grill top on it. Pretty soon the heat was spreading through the blind, and he put four plump hot dogs on to cook. While the meat warmed, we kept a look out for

ducks. As I was turning one of the dogs, Bill started calling. That meant ducks flying, so I froze.

A nice little wad of about a dozen mallards turned to the sound of Bill's calling and winged by to give us a look. I eased over to the front of the blind to get into shooting position. The ducks made another pass, but high and unconvinced. Bill pleaded with his call, and the birds swung wide, only to turn and come by again. There was something they didn't like, and they made another pass or two, still high and out of range. Despite Bill's best efforts, the ducks quit and went home.

We sat back on the bench and discussed the possible shortcomings of the blind or anything else that might have run the birds off. We had plenty of decoys, the wind was right, and we just couldn't figure out why these ducks refused to commit. As soon as you think you know how a wild animal will behave in a given situation, you're setting yourself up to be made a fool of. We decided that this bunch of ducks just didn't feel like stopping.

We'd only sat a minute or so when Bill spoke up. "Weren't there four hot dogs on that grill?" I looked

Duck Blind Dogs

over at the bucket and, sure enough, there were only three wieners on it. I searched around on the floor, thinking maybe I'd knocked one off the grill during the excitement of the duck calling. In my search, I looked down toward Tank's corner of the blind.

When we made eye contact, I heard that tail start to thump softly on the floor, and if a dog can be said to have a grin on his face, he had a big one. And then I knew. While Bill and I were absorbed with the circling mallards, the fearless black dog had left his post, filched a steaming wiener off that blistering grill, inhaled it and returned to his assigned corner. Only his lack of a poker face had betrayed him. If he was worried, the laughter of the duck hunters eased him.

So, in honor of the departed retriever, here's a recipe for Duck Blind Dogs:

INGREDIENTS: Two all-beef wieners (the big, thick ones) per person; sharp cheddar cheese; bacon slices, one per wiener; hot brown mustard.

Split the dogs down one side. Smear a little of the mustard in the slit and put a slice of cheese in, too. Now wrap a slice of bacon around the whole thing, pinning it down with toothpicks. Put the wieners on the grill, turning them often to prevent bacon from burning. Serve in a cold duck blind in the company of a good dog.

French French Toast

This one comes out of Durham's camp on Shedhorn Creek, where I cooked for the hunters and guides. It was a big hit at breakfast, and will really stick with you 'til lunch. With egg for protein, bread for carbohydrates, and fat from cooking oil, it makes a good, balanced meal.

Camp life has always suited me right down to the ground. I guess I could spend the rest of my life back up in the hills if the family would let me get away with it. This particular camp was situated in the Lee-Metcalf Wilderness in southwest Montana, and it was a real fine place to spend time. At the edge of the meadow, at about 8,000 feet, the view was outstanding, with the backside of Sphinx Mountain commanding the scene. I wish I was there right now.

The cook's job in a mountain hunting camp is a tough one, but satisfying, too. Unless he can con one of the guides into helping out, he's always first out of the sack to light the fires in the heating stoves of the cooking tent. I was lucky enough to have a propane range to cook on, but lots of cooks go wood all the way. Anyway, after firing the wood stoves, the next item is coffee, plenty strong and plenty of it. The smell of that brew will get the guides up, who in turn will wake the hunters. While the guides go out to wrangle the riding stock, the pilgrims come stumbling into the dining tent. A cup of "mud" keeps them going until the cook gets their breakfast ready.

In Durham's camp, after everybody was fed, mounted up, and off on the hunt, I'd put wash water on to heat and simmer the dishes for a while. At this point I'd usually catch a nap to make up for rising ahead of everybody else. When I rolled out again, a mountain of dirty dishes awaited. Once those were dealt with, there was always the log pile to be reduced to fire wood.

Before you get the idea that I was some sort of superman and did everything around camp, let me set the record straight. The guides, and sometimes even the hunters, pitched in to lend a hand. After supper, the guides would build the next day's lunches while I did dishes. Very often, one of them would do the drying. They also did the lion's share of the wood cutting and cared for the horses and mules. Add this to a ten-hour day out in the open, often in freezing weather, and you can see that their job was no cakewalk.

French French Toast

Every three or four days it would be necessary for someone to pack out meat or take unloaded mules down the mountain to be loaded with more camp supplies. As often as not, that job would fall to me, and it was my favorite duty. I'd cook up a couple of meals ahead of time and take off for the home ranch.

If there's anything better than travelling through the mountains on a good saddle horse, I've yet to find it. Though I made that ten-mile ride up and down the trail a whole slew of times, I never got tired of it. By the close of the season you could have bounced a bullet off the seat of my pants.

The roughest part of the job was watching all hands ride out every morning to take up the hunt while I stayed in camp. I felt like an old bird dog left in the kennel. But the day came when I had my chance. We've all heard stories about the big buck that wanders into camp while the hunters are gone, with old cookie still there doing the chores. And how old cookie lays down his dish towel and picks up his rifle, taking the buck from the door flap of the cook tent. Well, it happened to me.

One morning late in the season, with no one but me in camp, the buck we always hear about made his appearance. I was out in front of the cook tent, getting an armload of stove wood, and, like I usually did, had stopped to look out on the meadow. I spotted movement where the trail dropped over the rim of the clearing. It looked as if a pile of dead branches was climbing the hill.

Then the deer's head and neck came into view. It was no Boone and Crockett monster, but a nice, symmetrical four-pointer (western count), with its nose on the trail like an old hound dog. A doe in heat must have come up the trail earlier in the morning, and the buck was locked onto her scent. He either failed to see, or didn't care about, our camp.

As usual, I was in the market for meat. Laying the wood down as quietly as possible, I slipped backwards into the cook tent. Two or three rifles leaned against the wall. I grabbed the first one I could reach, a .270 belonging to one of the guides, and eased back outside. The buck was still coming, the distance about a hundred yards. As I braced my left hand against a tree to steady my shot, the deer

French French Toast

spotted my movement and left the trail. But the crosshairs were on him, and the job was done.

But back to French French Toast. It sounds like I'm stuttering, but it's called French French because it's made with French bread, so it's twice French. Here's how you fix it.

INGREDIENTS: One loaf French bread (sometimes I use sourdough, but it's a little tart); one egg per three slices toast; whole milk, one tablespoon per egg; powdered cinnamon; cooking oil.

Slice bread three-quarters to one inch thick. Break eggs in a bowl and whip to a froth. Add milk and whip some more. Dip slices in egg batter and place in lightly oiled skillet. (I like to pour some oil in a bowl and dip a paper towel in it, wiping the oiled towel over the cooking surface of the skillet. Too much oil will wreck your toast.) While the first side browns, shake a good dusting of powdered

cinnamon on the topside. Peek under the toast with your spatula, and when it's nicely browned, flip it over. Now spice the browned side.

Serve hot with bacon or sausage and you'll know your crew will be in good shape 'til lunch time.

Brace of Teal with Wild Rice

Those who know me also know my feelings toward waterfowl. They are the most graceful of birds. If they closed the duck and goose hunting season forever, I'd still go sit in a duck blind every fall to watch them fly. But the truth is that I love to hunt them. I love the birds, the boats, the decoys, the guns, the dogs, the calls, the blinds and everything that goes with wildfowling. But as much as anything else, I just love to eat wildfowl.

Different kinds of ducks vary in the quality of their flesh. Some, such as goldeneyes, are only passable fare and require a certain amount of chef's trickery to make them come up to standard. Others, like mallards and pintail, require nothing but a hot oven to do them justice. But above them all in delicate texture and flavor is the little teal.

Teal are small, about the size of a young pigeon. It takes two to make a meal for a hungry person, but laying hands on the makings of a teal dinner is not always easy. These little ducks fly like arrows, and connecting one with a load of coarse shot takes practice. Greenwing and bluewing teal are the most common, cinnamon teal the least prevalent. They are all food for the gods.

My first winter in Montana was marked by an abundance of duck hunting. I was single and working part time, so every chance that offered itself found me on the river or down at the lake. It was the first season for my first retriever, a little golden named Beau. It was also my first season of serious waterfowling, so the pup and I sort of trained each other. Between the two of us, we managed to put a few duck dinners on the table.

I didn't have any decoys that year, so I was compelled to get my ducks by jump shooting. That meant locating the birds while they rested or fed, then stalking within range and flushing them for the shot. There was also some pass shooting, where the pup and I would position ourselves along a flightline and take our chances as the ducks flew over. This is still one of my favorite methods of hunting; it offers very challenging shooting.

Brace of Teal with Wild Rice

My roommate that winter was a former chef from Colorado. He viewed my hunting with great interest, so I invited him to share a duck dinner with me. He accepted with gusto, and I began assembling the components: long grain white and wild rice, fresh broccoli, and, above all, the birds.

Beau and I had been lucky enough to take four green-winged teal home with us the day before, so I began prepping them for the night's supper. They were already drawn and picked, so I rinsed them carefully and set them to one side and went on to deal with other aspects of the meal. My roommate's cat, a big black and white male named Easy, had watched my every move with fascination. I suspected his intentions were less than honorable, so I ran him out of the kitchen.

I went to the pantry for something, probably garlic (I never seem to have enough garlic). When I came back to the kitchen, only three ducks were on the drain board. For some reason, I didn't immediately suspect the cat. I asked my roommate if he had picked it up.

He hadn't. When I turned back to the sink, I saw Easy streaking across the bathroom floor with a second duck in his mouth. He was almost under the tub when I got hold of his tail and dragged him back out. He hung onto the duck, and I'm sure that's all that saved me from a nasty bite.

After changing my grip to the back of his neck, I managed to pry the duck from his jaws. This time I heaved him outside. The first duck to disappear was also under the tub. If the damned cat hadn't been so greedy trying for the second bird, he might have gotten away with it.

The two ducks Easy had snatched were a little chewed, and since the cat was responsible, his owner got those two birds. He never seemed to notice, and if he did, he never spoke up. In any case, the meal was outstanding, and here's the recipe for Brace of Teal with Wild Rice.

INGREDIENTS: Brace (two) teal per person; four-ounce package of wild rice; one cup long-grain white rice; olive oil; garlic cloves, crushed; 1/4 fresh lemon.

Brace of Teal with Wild Rice

Rinse the birds thoroughly, especially if they've been chewed on by a cat, and pat dry. Rub outside of each bird with olive oil, then with crushed garlic. Place ducks in roaster, uncovered, and place in 500-degree oven for fifteen minutes. Leave the body cavities unstuffed to allow heat to enter. Teal are small and cook quickly.

Fix wild rice according to directions on the package. For the long-grain white rice, boil two cups of water and dump in one cup of rice. Stir well and turn down to simmer. Forty minutes to an hour will do. When both kinds of rice are done, mix them together and melt some butter over all. The juice of $1/4$ lemon goes in now. Stir it up to blend. If you like, prepare the dipping sauce found in the recipe for Roast Wild Duck. Serve with asparagus or broccoli or whatever green veggie you prefer.

Grandpa Gander Fillets

Like the bass fisherman bragging up the "hawg" largemouth he caught last weekend, the goose hunter wants everyone to know when he takes a big honker. But, too often, the fun stops when that monster bird gets to the dinner table. Really large geese, say those over ten pounds dressed weight, are usually older birds and can be pretty chewy. If they're oven roasted as you'd do a young bird, you may wind up with a jaw breaker for your main course.

One of the first geese I ever brought home was a whopping twelve-pounder. I roasted him the conventional way. The gravy was tender, but the meat had to be diced up for soup. After two days of simmering, the soup even got tender.

The simple solution would be to shoot only young birds, but when the Canadas are coming into the decoy spread and the shotguns start to pop, it's hard to screen your targets. Better to take your chances as they come, and if you get a Grandpa Gander, treat him special like this:

INGREDIENTS: One wild goose over ten pounds dressed weight; one cup olive oil; two cups red wine; two tablespoons red wine vinegar; two crushed garlic cloves.

Don't bother to pick a goose this large. Skin it. Bone out both halves of the breast. (Dice up the rest of the bird for soup or hash.) Slice the breast fillets, across the grain of the meat, into $1/4$-inch strips. Combine all other ingredients in a large bowl and put the sliced meat in. Marinate overnight.

To cook, drain off the marinade and pat meat dry with paper towels. Melt enough butter to cover the bottom of a good-sized skillet. Get skillet hot, but not smoking hot, and quickly pan fry the slices, turning them after about a minute. Serve medium to medium rare. Salt and pepper to taste.

Wilderness Ethics

"Nature cannot be improved upon. We can change it, embellish it, and twist it to our purpose, but we can't make it better. True wilderness is as close to perfection as can be found on this earth. What the Creator has made, we can only alter."

Quite a mouthful from an old camp cook, eh? But it's the "By God truth!" There is precious little wild land left on this planet, and it gets to be less all the time. If we want to keep it, we have to take care of it. Just as there are ethics for behavior in business and daily living, there are ethics for us to follow when we enter wilderness areas.

If you can sum it up into one sentence, it's this: Leave every campsite looking like you had never been there. That was the code of my Scoutmaster, and it works just as well today as it did thirty years ago. Nothing infuriates me more than to spend hard time and sweat to get back into a remote area only to find that some ill-bred lowlife has trashed up the country by leaving a messy campsite. There is simply no excuse for that sort of thing, unless ignorance and stupidity qualify.

Now, I'll get off my soapbox and share some tips for treading lightly on the wilderness. First, don't spend forever in one place. No matter how low-impact your philosophy, your camp will get that "lived in" look after awhile. Move around, see new country. If possible, use an established site rather than pioneering a new one.

When it comes to firewood, use good judgment. If you're in an area that gets few visitors, and dead trees and dry brush are in good supply, then have a sure enough fire. But when above timberline or in a heavy traffic area, carry a gas stove such as a Primus or butane cartridge model. And remember that standing dead trees provide homes for birds and small mammals, so use the downfall timber first.

Regarding trash, if you can pack it in, you can pack it out. The old practice of burying flattened cans and other garbage won't cut it anymore. The wilderness doesn't need mini-landfills. It's okay to burn some things, like paper, egg shells, and other items that are consumed completely, but plastics usually wind up in a glob of molten debris if thrown in the fire. Think about this when you choose the stuff you carry on your trip.

Wilderness Ethics

Concerning sanitary procedure, a lot of little catholes are preferable to one big latrine. And when you dig those holes, stay well away from streams and lake shores. In one camp I cooked for, a hunter actually defecated within a foot of our water source. He didn't bother to dig a hole. He also went down the mountain the next day. Make those holes shallow, as waste matter decomposes much faster in the topsoil layer than down in the clay.

When packing in with horses and mules, certain practices should be observed. Don't tie stock to young trees for long periods. The animals will pace around and around the trunks, rubbing the bark raw with the halter rope. And don't picket animals overnight by tying them to big trees; they'll paw and stomp and damage the roots. Instead, tie a high line between two trees and above the animals' heads, and then tie each halter rope to the high line. Leave enough space between the stock so they don't bicker.

Finally, care for the wilderness as if it were your lover. There's little enough left, and nobody's making any more. Go often to visit, but don't try to make it home. It's too special, too fragile. Behave like a privileged guest because that's what you are. Wilderness is ours to see and enjoy, but it belongs to itself.

Epilogue: A Final Word . . . Or Two

Since you're at this end of the book, I'll give myself the benefit of the doubt and assume you started at the other end, and possibly even read it. If so, I hope you found something in it you like. If you're skimming, buy it.

I also hope that by reading these stories you've had your appetite whetted for some outdoor adventure. Saddle a horse and take to the hills. Joint up your flyrod and wade into some fast, cold water. Take your Lab and your pump gun and go see if those northern birds are down yet. Have some fun.

And while you're out there having yourself some fun, take a little time to think about what you're doing. Whether you are hunting, fishing, hiking, camping, canoeing, horse packing or whatever, the resource is limited and your enemies are many. Legions of developers, exploiters, and polluters of every stripe stand ready to buy, sell, and pave over the last square foot of Mother Earth. She's taken a hell of a beating in the last fifty years, and if she's going to pull through, she needs a helping hand. Ponder on what you, on an individual basis, might be able to do. Then do it.

I hope you understand that it's not always necessary to fill your creel or game bag to enjoy your days afield. We Americans are way too consumption oriented. When we put our emphasis on dead fish, ducks, deer and other game, we miss all the good stuff. Open your eyes. Listen. Smell. Chew on a grass stem. The birds, fish or whatever will still be there.

Finally, I hope you'll try some of my recipes. One or two of them could result in something good to eat.

John R. Wright
Durango, Colorado
January 1991

About the Author

ED ABRAHAMSON

Chef Shedhorn, a.k.a. John Wright, has spent a life outdoors. Raised in Tennessee, he has lived most of his adult life in the mountains of the West. All his free time has been spent hunting, fishing, riding, skiing, and backpacking in the Rockies, Sierras, and North Cascades.

At different times, he has worked as a carpenter, surveyor, ranch hand, cartoonist, hunting guide, camp cook and cowboy. He lives in Durango, Colorado with his wife, son, and a Labrador retriever.